TECTUM
PUBLISHERS

Tectum Publishers of Style

© 2009 Tectum Publishers NV
Godefriduskaai 22
2000 Antwerp
Belgium
p +32 3 226 66 73
f +32 3 226 53 65
info@ tectum.be
www.tectum.be

ISBN: 978-907976-11-04
WD: 2009/9021/14
(77)

© 2009 edited and content creation by fusion publishing GmbH Berlin
www.fusion-publishing.com
info@fusion-publishing.com

Team: Martin Joachim (Idea), Dirk Alt (Editor), Kerstin Klose (Visual concept), Bianca Maria Öller (Introduction, texts), Mariel Marohn
(Editorial coordination), Friederike Krump (Assistance), Janine Minkner (Layout), Peter Fritzsche (Imaging & Pre-press),
Sabine Scholz (Text coordination), Dr. Suzanne Kirkbright – Artes Translations

English translation by Artes Translation: Conan Kirkpatrick
French translation by Artes Translation: Brigitte Villaumié
Dutch translation by M&M translation: Michel Mathijs

Cover photo: Getty Images
Back cover photos from top to bottom: Associated Press, courtesy www.iwantoneofthose.com, courtesy Stamp Collection AG

Printed in China

ama⅃ing 02

auctions

TECTUM
PUBLISHERS

IN
EVERYONE
WILL

FOR

THE FUTURE,

BE
FAMOUS
15 MINUTES.

ANDY WARHOL (1928–1987)
AMERICAN ARTIST

intro

Attending an auction is about more than just buying something. The uncertainty of how high the closing bid will be and the anticipation of perhaps outbidding your rivals for the object of your desire—it is these emotions that turn any auction into an enticing and captivating game. Great demand for an object can lead to exorbitant prices and, indeed, to some dramatic split-second decisions. After all, where else can you bid for one-of-a-kind artifacts, objects of historical value or rare collector's items?

All these unusual, sometimes outrageously expensive and desirable objects are at the heart of *Amazing Auctions*, including the Wittelsbach Diamond, which changed hands for more than $ 24 million, and the world's most expensive stamp. And that's not all! You'll also learn about auction items of the curious kind, such as a slice of toast bearing the likeness of the Holy Virgin Mary, the world's most expensive phone number, a cornflake shaped like the state of Illinois, and even unusual locations such as an entire jail.

Some of the insights into the fascinating world of auctions may leave you shaking your head and dropping your jaw in amazement, or even feeling a tinge of jealousy at outbidders who were able to come into possession of some very special objects. In any case, though, *Amazing Auctions* really makes you want to feel the excitement of an auction live—and even to do some bidding of your own one day!

Participer à une vente aux enchères, ce n'est pas seulement acquérir un objet. La tension de ne pas savoir jusqu'où vont monter les enchères et l'excitation de se demander si l'on va vraiment pouvoir emporter l'objet désiré sont des émotions fortes qui font d'une vente aux enchères une fascinante et captivante compétition. Une enchère très disputée peut aboutir à des prix faramineux et des cas de conscience dramatiques. Car c'est bien à l'occasion de ventes aux enchères que sont souvent offerts des pièces uniques exceptionnelles, des antiquités historiques de grande valeur et des objets de collection rares.

Amazing Auctions présente précisément ces objets exceptionnels très convoités, parfois affreusement chers, comme par exemple le diamant connu sous le nom de « Der Blaue Wittelsbacher » qui a changé de main pour la somme de 24 millions de dollars, ou le timbre le plus précieux au monde. On trouve également des curiosités vendues aux enchères telles qu'un toast à l'effigie de la Vierge Marie, le numéro de téléphone le plus cher du monde, un corn-flake aux contours de l'État américain de l'Illinois ou des bâtiments particuliers comme toute une prison.

Cet aperçu du monde étrange des enchères nous fait peut-être quelquefois hocher la tête de désapprobation, nous laisse médusés et nous rend, qui sait, parfois un peu jaloux de ces enchérisseurs qui ont pu s'offrir des objets d'exception. *Amazing Auctions* nous donne assurément très envie d'assister à l'une de ces ventes pour ressentir personnellement le frisson des enchères – et pourquoi pas enchérir à notre tour !

Een veiling bijwonen gaat over meer dan kopen alleen. De onzekerheid over hoe hoog het uiteindelijke bod zal uitvallen en de hoop je concurrenten voor het voorwerp van je dromen te overtroeven, dat zijn de emoties die van een veiling een aanlokkelijk en opwindend spel maken. Wanneer er grote vraag is naar een bepaald object, kan dit tot exorbitante prijzen en, ja, soms ook dramatische, in een fractie van een seconde te nemen beslissingen leiden. Want waar anders zou je kunnen bieden op unieke artefacten, voorwerpen van historische waarde of zeldzame verzamelitems?

Al deze ongewone, soms waanzinnig dure en vaak begerenswaardige objecten staan centraal in *Amazing Auctions*, waaronder ook de Wittelsbach Diamant, die voor meer dan 24 miljoen $ van eigenaar veranderde, en 's werelds duurste postzegel. En dat is nog niet alles! U zult ook kunnen lezen over veilingitems van een wat vreemdere soort zoals een snee toast met de vermeende beeltenis van de Heilige Maagd Maria, 's werelds duurste telefoonnummer, een cornflake in de vorm van de Amerikaanse staat Illinois en zelfs ongewone locaties zoals een hele gevangenis.

Bij een aantal verhalen over de fascinerende veilingwereld zal u wellicht eens het hoofd schudden, bij andere zult u bijna achterover vallen van verbazing of misschien zelfs een tikje jaloers worden op bieders die wel heel bijzondere voorwerpen wisten te bemachtigen. Wat er ook van zij, *Amazing Auctions* zal u in elk geval zin geven om het opwindende van een veiling ook eens live mee te maken en, waarom niet, zelf eens te bieden!

contents

rich and beautiful   01

happy birthday, mr. president // a little piece of cloth with plenty sex appeal // jimi hendrix as up close as it gets //
the white album no. 0000005 // what a scary passport // holiday with mr. bean // here to save the world //
elvis presley's peacock outfit // a guide to marilyn's companions // join the sgt. pepper's lonely hearts club band //
dress up for a breakfast at tiffany's // no new queen for marie antoinette's pearls // the wittelsbach diamond //
let's play bonnie and clyde // to be as cool as james bond // ursula, undress! // k.i.t.t. and michael part ways //
fight against darth vader // worth every penny // the first lady of france—in the buff // cher's black little nothing //
che guevara's revolutionary bangs

expensive   02

a true classic—the bugatti royale // double eagle—the most expensive coin // allah's words of immeasurable value //
the violin of the devil's fiddler // the most expensive fossil // the magic price for words // the most expensive scrabble board //
what time is it? // the most expensive baseball card // a very personal declaration of independence //
the first adventure of spiderman // sex.com for millions of dollars // a very special license plate // 5 £ + auction = $ 31,200 //
the most expensive bottle of wine // white truffles—edible gold // andy warhol meets velvet underground //
pablo picasso's masterpiece // the world's most expensive cow // the most expensive stamp ever

curiosities   03

my holy toast // the beautiful teeth of paris hilton // there's money in cornflakes // chocolate from the south pole //
britney's real gum back // a royal piece of cake // royal stockings from way back when // not tonight, josephine //
what nobody needs // the luckiest phone number ever: 8x8 // what a good old beer // beam me up, scotty! //
make love not war // a kid named erich honecker // adolf hitler's globe // look into the future with nostradamus //
it's magic: houdini's water torture cell // buying drugs from the government // katie's top model hairstyle //
a "holy" car—the pope's vw golf // one key could have saved them all // whole life for sale

locations   04

my home is my prison // the wall must go // room for a real mega party // my home, my car, my hamlet //
how big: galaxy for sale // the minsk—a giant of the seven seas // be a part of disneyland—on a tombstone //
a window that changed world history // stairway to heaven // anybody want to buy belgium? // big wheel keeps on turning //
your name on mount mckinley // the sexiest millennium party ever

01 happy birthday, mr. president!

October 1999, Christie's, New York USA

$1,267,500

Who can ever forget what has to be the most seductive birthday serenade of all times—Marilyn Monroe singing to President John F. Kennedy in 1962. On the occasion of her sensational appearance, the blonde diva had a silk dress tailored precisely to her dimensions—skin-tight with the color of flesh. Given how it made history that day, it comes as no surprise that this glamour gown sold for more than 1 million dollars at Christie's Auction House by the year 1999!

Le monde entier, ou presque, se rappelle aujourd'hui encore la sérénade le plus érotique de tous les temps que Marilyn Monroe chanta en 1962 à l'occasion de l'anniversaire du président américain John F. Kennedy. Pour cette sensationnelle entrée en scène, la blonde actrice s'était fait coudre à même le corps une robe fourreau en gaze de soie couleur chair. Pas étonnant que cette tenue glamour empreinte d'histoire ait dépassé le million de dollars lors de sa vente aux enchères chez Christie's en 1999.

Wie herinnert zich de meest verleidelijke verjaardagsserenade van alle tijden niet: Marilyn Monroe die in 1962 zingt voor President John F. Kennedy. Tijdens haar sensationele verschijning droeg de blonde diva een zijden jurk, handgemaakt naar haar perfecte afmetingen, heel nauwsluitend en in huidskleur. Gezien alle commotie en de geschiedenis van deze sensationele lange jurk, mag het niet verwonderen dat ze tijdens een veiling bij Christie's in 1999 voor meer dan 1 miljoen dollar de deur uit ging!

a little piece of cloth with plenty sex appeal

October 2005, eBay online

© Getty Images

$13,860

With her lascivious music videos and expensive, sexy stage shows, singer Kylie Minogue roused millions of fans around the globe at the turn of the millennium. It was all the more dramatic when the erotic pop star developed breast cancer. But even as Kylie Minogue was dealing with the resulting long-term treatments, she was already doing her part to help women with breast cancer. For example, when she gave away her sexy black-and-pink favorite bra to a charity auction.

Avec ses vidéos musicales sensuelles et ses shows aux mises en scène torrides et sophistiquées, la chanteuse Kylie Minogue déchaîna les passions chez les hommes et les femmes de par le monde, au passage du nouveau millénaire. C'est pourquoi ce fut un drame quand la voluptueuse star fut atteinte d'un cancer du sein. Alors qu'elle était en train de subir de longs traitements, elle fit tout pour apporter son soutien à d'autres femmes atteintes d'un cancer du sein. C'est ainsi qu'elle remit son soutien-gorge préféré, noir et rose vif très sexy, à une vente aux enchères de charité.

Met haar wulpse muziekvideo's en dure, sexy podiumshows wond Kylie Minogue eind vorige eeuw miljoenen fans op over de hele wereld. Des te dramatischer was het toen bij de erotische popster borstkanker werd vastgesteld. Maar terwijl Kylie Minogue zich nog door de lange behandelingen worstelde, droeg ze al haar steentje bij om vrouwen met borstkanker te helpen. Zo gaf ze bijvoorbeeld haar favoriete, sexy zwart-met-roze beha aan een veiling voor het goede doel.

jimi hendrix as up close as it gets

July 2008, Christie's, London UK

$ 39,580

Whether those red-olive-blue-green-striped pants from the Flower-Power era would still set accents today seems rather doubtful. What we do know, however, is that this one-of-a-kind garment was worn by the wildest and possibly best guitarist of all times: Jimi Hendrix. In July 2008, the hippies-for-life and the collectors of Rock 'n' Roll memorabilia among us were presented with the opportunity to buy this piece of Rock history at an auction at Christie's in London—where it met its new owner for a price of $ 39,580.

Ce pantalon hippie rayé rouge, olive, bleu et vert, en laine mélangée, ne risque guère d'inspirer la mode d'aujourd'hui. On sait par contre que ce vêtement unique en son genre fut porté par le plus fou et peut-être le meilleur guitariste de tous les temps : Jimi Hendrix. En juillet 2008, les anciens hippies et collectionneurs de souvenirs des années rock et pop purent enchérir sur ce morceau d'histoire de la musique chez Christie's à Londres – il fut adjugé pour 39 580 dollars à un nouvel amateur.

Of zo'n rood, olijfgroen, blauw en groen gestreepte broeken uit de flowerpowertijd ook vandaag nog zouden scoren, daar hebben we onze twijfels over. Wat we wel weten, is dat dit best wel unieke kledingstuk werd gedragen door de wildste en mogelijk beste gitarist aller tijden, Jimi Hendrix. In juli 2008 kregen de levenslange hippies onder ons en verzamelaars van rock 'n' roll memorabilia de gelegenheid om dit stukje rockgeschiedenis bij Christie's in Londen te kopen – de nieuwe eigenaar had er alvast $ 39.580 voor over.

the white album no. 0000005

November 2008, eBay online

$30,000

The BEATLES

0000005

The Beatles' "White Album" sold more than 19 million copies worldwide. Any of those copies in and of themselves may not seem remarkable in any way, but when No. 0000005 went up or sale, whispers started going around among vinyl collectors. The first four serial numbers of the album belong to the four Beatles—John Lennon, Paul McCartney, George Harrison and Ringo Starr. Therefore, No. 0000005 is the lowest edition of the album on the market, which makes it No. 1 among the rarest vinyl records in the world.

L'album blanc des Beatles fut vendu dans le monde entier à plus de 19 millions d'exemplaires. A première vue, ce disque n'a donc rien d'extraordinaire. Mais quand la version vinyle frappée du n° de série 0000005 fut mise en vente, la nouvelle se répandit comme une traînée de poudre parmi les collectionneurs de disques : les quatre premiers exemplaires de l'album ayant été remis aux quatre Beatles, John Lennon, Paul McCartney, George Harrison et Ringo Starr, le n° de série 0000005 est donc le premier exemplaire sur le marché et classé comme l'album le plus rare de tous les temps.

Van "The White Album" van The Beatles werden wereldwijd meer dan 19 miljoen exemplaren verkocht. Een gewoon exemplaar hiervan is op zich dan ook niet zo bijzonder, maar toen album nr. 0000005 te koop werd aangeboden, gaf dit aanleiding tot nogal wat commotie onder vinylverzamelaars. De eerste vier serienummers van het album behoren namelijk toe aan de vier Beatles zelf – John Lennon, Paul McCartney, George Harrison en Ringo Starr. Album nr. 0000005 is dan ook de laagste op de markt verkrijgbare editie en dus nummer 1 van een van de meest bijzondere vinylplaten ter wereld.

$ 19,200

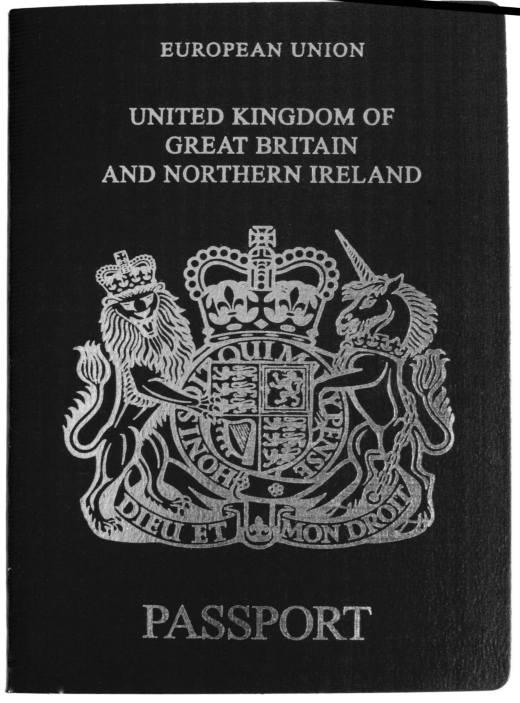

EUROPEAN UNION

UNITED KINGDOM OF
GREAT BRITAIN
AND NORTHERN IRELAND

PASSPORT

"Dial M for Murder", "Rear Window", "Psycho" and "Birds"—who doesn't know the famous film classics by Alfred Hitchcock. His unique work as a director, which combined suspense with humor, introduced new ways of filmmaking and which also helped him leave his mark as a movie director, remains an influence on numerous filmmakers to this day. Hence, it's safe to assume that several of his loyal fans were there in June 2007 when the West Hollywood based auction house Julien's put up Hitchcock's passport for auction. One of them bought the valuable document for more than $ 19,000.

« Le crime était presque parfait », « Fenêtre sur cour », « Psychose », « Les oiseaux » – qui ne connaît pas ces grands classiques d'Alfred Hitchcock. Sa réalisation singulière, mêlant suspense et humour, qui introduisit des moyens cinématographiques innovants et qui le faisait même apparaître dans le film, influence aujourd'hui encore nombre de cinéastes. Quand le passeport d'Hitchcock fut vendu aux enchères en juin 2007 par la maison de vente Julien's à West Hollywood, quelques fans fidèles étaient assurément présents. L'un d'eux fit l'acquisition du précieux passeport pour plus de 19 000 dollars.

"Dial M for Murder", "Rear Window", "Psycho" en "Birds" – wie kent er niet de beroemde filmklassiekers van Alfred Hitchcock? Zijn unieke werk als regisseur, waarbij hij suspense met humor combineerde, betekende het startschot van een nieuwe manier om films te maken en hielp hem ook om zijn stempel te drukken als filmregisseur. Ook vandaag nog heeft dit een invloed op tal van filmmakers. Men kan dan ook gerust stellen dat verschillende trouwe fans in juni van 2007 op post waren toen veilinghuis Julien's in West Hollywood het paspoort van Hitchcock veilde. Een van die fans kocht het waardevolle document voor meer dan $ 19.000.

March 2007, eBay online

$ 2,055

Whatever Mr. Bean does, it has a way of ending in disaster. Well, it's no different in his hilarious blockbuster "Mr. Bean's Holiday", which finds the clumsy Englishman traveling through France after winning in the lottery. His only companion on his journey is an old-fashioned suitcase made of brown leather and checkered material. In time for the movie's debut in German movie theaters, that suitcase was sold on eBay Germany for charitable purposes. As a result of the sale, the original prop changed ownership for $ 2,055.

Quoi que Mr. Bean fasse, cela ne peut finir qu'en catastrophe. C'est encore le cas dans le film comique « Les vacances de Mr. Bean », dans lequel notre Anglais pataud gagne un voyage en France lors d'une tombola. Pendant son voyage, il est accompagné d'une valise démodée en cuir brun et doublure à carreaux. Juste au moment de la sortie du film en salles en Allemagne, la valise fut vendue aux enchères sur le site allemand d'eBay au profit d'une œuvre caritative : cet accessoire original y trouva un nouveau propriétaire pour 2 055 dollars.

Wat Mr. Bean ook doet, het eindigt bijna altijd in een catastrofe. Dat is ook niet anders in zijn hilarische blockbuster "Mr. Bean's Holiday", waarin de onhandige Engelsman na het winnen van de lotto doorheen Frankrijk trekt. Zijn enige compagnon op deze reis is een ouderwetse koffer in bruin leer met dambordpatroon. Naar aanleiding van de première van de film in de Duitse filmzalen werd deze koffer op eBay Duitsland voor het goede doel verkocht. Het resultaat van de veiling: het originele rekwisiet verwisselde van eigenaar voor $ 2.055.

© Getty Images

here to save the world

July 2003, Profiles in History, Calabasas Hills USA

$ 126,500

To many, he was the real Superman—George Reeves, who portrayed the popular comic figure in the series "Adventures of Superman" from 1952 to 1958. The costume that turned him into the superhero from planet Krypton in the studio was auctioned off in the year 2003. After one of the only two costumes in existence was badly damaged, the experts at the auction house Profiles in History put the valuable second one up for sale, which brought them the enormous sum of $ 126,500.

Beaucoup le considèrent comme le vrai Superman : Georges Reeves, qui incarna de 1952 à 1958 le héros populaire de la série des Aventures de Superman. Le costume qui fit de lui au cinéma le super héros de la planète Crypton fut mis à prix en 2003. L'un des deux seuls costumes existants ayant été gravement endommagé, les spécialistes de la maison de ventes aux enchères Profiles in History mirent en vente le précieux deuxième exemplaire et en obtinrent la somme mirifique de 126 500 dollars.

Voor velen was hij de echte Superman: George Reeves, de man die de populaire stripfiguur van 1952 tot 1958 gestalte gaf in de serie "De avonturen van Superman". Het pak dat hem transformeerde tot superheld van de planeet Krypton werd geveild in 2003. Nadat een van de slechts twee bestaande kostuums ernstig werd beschadigd, boden de experts van het veilinghuis 'Profiles in History' het waardevolle tweede pak ter veiling aan, wat hun de enorme som van $ 126.500 opbracht.

elvis presley's peacock outfit

August 2008, GOTTA HAVE IT!® Collectibles, New York USA

$ 300,000

Elvis Presley was an outstanding musician, a popular actor, a sensational entertainer—and a trendsetter in fashion and style. His hairstyle—the typical ducktail and wide sideburns—is imitated to this day. His outrageous suits and outfits remain synonymous to that uniquely new, male stage presence. And nothing exemplifies this better than Elvis's much beloved peacock costume: A skintight overall with an opulent belt and carefully embroidered peacock motive, which sold for $ 300,000 at an auction.

Elvis Presley était un fabuleux musicien, un acteur adulé, un animateur sensationnel – et un faiseur de tendance en matière de mode et de style. Sa coiffure typique avec toupet et larges rouflaquettes est encore imitée aujourd'hui. Ses costumes débridés et ses tenues de scène excentriques sont la marque d'une présence scénique particulièrement virile jamais vue auparavant. L'exemple le plus emblématique est la tenue de scène préférée d'Elvis : une combinaison moulante ornée d'une opulente ceinture, figurant un paon richement brodé, qui fut vendue aux enchères pour 300 000 dollars.

Elvis Presley was een begenadigd muzikant, een populaire acteur, een sensationele entertainer – en een trendsetter op het gebied van mode en stijl. Zijn kapsel – met de typische 'eendenstaart' en brede bakkebaarden – vindt ook nu nog navolging. Zijn extravagante pakken en outfits blijven synoniem met die unieke, nieuwe, mannelijke verschijning op het podium. En daar is geen beter voorbeeld van dan Elvis' alom geliefde pauwenkostuum: een nauw aansluitende overall met een rijkelijk versierde broeksriem en zorgvuldig geborduurd pauwenmotief, dat voor $ 300.000 van de hand ging op een veiling

a guide to marilyn's companions

June 2005, Julien's Auctions, West Hollywood USA

Montgomery Clift, Joe DiMaggio, Henry Fonda, Hedda Hopper, Peter Lawford, Jack Lemmon, Arthur Miller, Jane Russell, Frank Sinatra, Lee & Paula Strasberg—and a score of other famous names, all in alphabetical order: Marilyn Monroe's personal little phone number book from 1962 has 'em all. It's a treasure for all those yearning for the memories of the celebrities and great artists of the 1960s. In June 2005, it was auctioned off at the bargain price of $ 90,000 at Julien's in West Hollywood.

Montgomery Clift, Joe DiMaggio, Henry Fonda, Hedda Hopper, Peter Lawford, Jack Lemmon, Arthur Miller, Jane Russell, Frank Sinatra, Lee & Paula Strasberg – et bien d'autres noms célèbres, classés par ordre alphabétique : le classique petit répertoire téléphonique de Marilyn Monroe datant de 1962 les contient tous. Une aubaine inespérée pour tous ceux qui suivent les traces des célébrités et des grands artistes des années 60. En juin 2005, l'acquéreur chez Julien's à West Hollywood fit une bonne affaire pour 90 000 dollars.

Montgomery Clift, Joe DiMaggio, Henry Fonda, Hedda Hopper, Peter Lawford, Jack Lemmon, Arthur Miller, Jane Russell, Frank Sinatra, Lee & Paula Strasberg – en nog een heleboel andere beroemde namen, allemaal in alfabetische volgorde: ze zijn allemaal te vinden in Marilyn Monroe's persoonlijk telefoonboekje uit 1962. Het is een ware schat voor iedereen die hunkert naar de herinneringen aan de grote sterren en artiesten van de jaren 1960. In juni 2005 werd het boekje voor het luttele bedrag van $ 90.000 bij Julien's in West Hollywood geveild.

CHRISTIE'S

join the sgt. pepper's lonely hearts club band

July 2008, Christie's, London UK

$1,071,133

The first thing the Sgt. Pepper's Lonely Hearts Club Band brings to mind is the Beatles and their brilliant, groundbreaking music. And let's not forget all the pictures that went with it, like the wild album cover, the Beatles in their colorful garments—oh, and the drum set with all the writing on it. And it was exactly that psychedelically embroidered drum that went up for auction at Christie's in London in July 2008. Thanks to its vast demand, the Flower Power Drum sold for the magical price of over $ 1 million.

Quand on pense au Sgt. Pepper's Lonely Hearts Club Band, on se rappelle d'abord les Beatles et leur musique tellement géniale et novatrice. Et l'on revoit tout de suite les images qui vont avec : une couverture d'album farfelue, les Beatles dans des costumes bariolés – sans oublier le tambour peint à la main. C'est précisément la peau de cette grosse caisse au design psychédélique qui fut mise en vente en juillet 2008 chez Christie's à Londres. La compétition ayant été enfiévrée, ce tambour qui a marqué le mouvement « Flower Power » atteignit la somme fabuleuse de plus d'un million de dollars.

Het eerste waar je aan denkt bij 'Sgt. Pepper's Lonely Hearts Club Band' zijn de Beatles en hun schitterende, grensverleggende muziek. En laten we ook niet de vele tekeningen vergeten die ermee gepaard gingen, zoals de wilde albumcover met de Beatles in hun kleurrijke kledij en – oh, ja – het drumstel met al die dingen erop geschreven. Het was precies dit drumstel dat bij Christie's in Londen in juli 2008 werd geveild. Dankzij de enorme belangstelling ging de flowerpowerdrum uiteindelijk onder de hamer voor de magische prijs van meer dan $ 1 miljoen.

dress up for a breakfast at tiffany's

December 2006, Christie's, London UK

$923,187

"Breakfast at Tiffany's" by Truman Capote was already a highly successful novel. In its movie version, with Audrey Hepburn as the main cast, the story of petite Holly Golightly took the whole world by storm in the early 1960s. And Audrey Hepburn, in her little black dress, became an icon of style to a whole generation of young women. Often copied, the original dress went up for auction for charitable purposes in December 2006. Its selling price, north of $ 900,000, benefited impoverished children in India.

« Petit déjeuner chez Tiffany », le roman de Truman Capote avait déjà remporté un vif succès. Portée à l'écran avec Audrey Hepburn dans le rôle principal, l'histoire de la fantasque Holly Golightly conquit le monde entier au début des années 60. Dans sa petite robe noire, Audrey Hepburn devint une icône de style pour toute une génération de jeunes femmes. L'original de cette robe si souvent copiée fut vendu en décembre 2006 au profit d'une organisation humanitaire. Les 900 000 dollars de recette vinrent en aide aux enfants défavorisés en Inde.

Het boek "Breakfast at Tiffany's" van Truman Capote was op zich al een heel succesvolle roman, maar de filmversie, met Audrey Hepburn als hoofdrolspeelster in het verhaal van de tengere Holly Golightly, veroverde in het begin van de jaren '60 de hele wereld. En maakte van Audrey Hepburn, in haar zwarte jurkje, een stijlicoon voor een hele generatie jonge vrouwen. De originele jurk, die vaak werd gekopieerd, ging in december 2006 onder de hamer voor het goede doel. De opbrengst, meer dan $ 900.000, ging naar arme Indiase kinderen.

no new queen for marie antoinette's pearls

December 2007, Christie's, London UK, unsold

$700,000

Marie-Antoinette is a striking figure in French history. The Queen of the French Revolution, who died at the guillotine, loved the finer aspects of life. This eternally young beauty had a penchant for the latest fashion, extravagant hairstyles and luxurious jewelry. One particularly unique trinket of diamonds, rubies and pearls was up for auction at Christie's in December 2007. To date, however, no one has been willing to come up with the money for the asking price of $ 700,000.

Marie-Antoinette est un personnage chatoyant de l'histoire de France. La Reine de la révolution française, qui fut exécutée sur l'échafaud, était amoureuse des belles choses de la vie. Habillée à la dernière mode, portant des coiffures originales et de luxueux bijoux, elle avait la passion de la beauté et de la jeunesse éternelles. Une parure de bijoux exceptionnelle faite de diamants, rubis et perles devait être vendue aux enchères en décembre 2007 chez Christie's. Pourtant, jusqu'à maintenant, personne ne fut disposé à payer les 700 000 dollars de mise à prix.

Marie-Antoinette is een opvallende figuur uit de Franse geschiedenis. De koningin van de Franse Revolutie, die onder de guillotine stierf, hield van de goede dingen des levens. Deze eeuwig jonge schoonheid was gesteld op de laatste mode, extravagante kapsels en luxueuze juwelen. In december van 2007 werd een bijzonder uniek kleinood met diamanten, robijnen en parels geveild bij Christie's. Maar tot op heden heeft nog niemand de vraagprijs van $ 700.000 op tafel gelegd.

© Getty Images

the wittelsbach diamond

December 2008, Christie's, London UK

$ 24,311,191

It's a big blue diamond weighing 35.56 Karats and absolutely unique—the Wittelsbach Diamond. In the past, it commanded the respect of the people of Bavaria—prominently displayed on the crown of the Bavarian king. By 1951, the precious diamond was still in the ownership of the Wittelsbach clan. Then the rare gem was sold and disappeared without a trace until it reemerged in December 2008 at Christie's where a London jeweler purchased it for more than $ 24 million.

C'est un gros diamant bleu, absolument unique, pesant 35,56 carats et connu sous le nom de « Der Blaue Wittelsbacher ». Par le passé, cette pierre était comme un phare pour le peuple bavarois – incrustée à la place d'honneur sur la couronne du Roi de Bavière. Le précieux diamant resta la propriété des Wittelsbach jusqu'en 1951. Après sa vente, on perdit sa trace jusqu'à ce que ce joyau rarissime ressurgisse en décembre 2008 où il fut acheté aux enchères chez Christie's par un joaillier londonien pour un prix historique de plus de 24 millions de dollars.

De Wittelsbach Diamant – een grote, blauwe diamant die 35,56 karaat weegt en absoluut uniek is. Vroeger dwong hij het respect af van de inwoners van Beieren – als opvallend juweel op de kroon van de koning van Beieren. Tot 1951 was de kostbare diamant nog altijd in het bezit van de Wittelsbach clan. Daarna werd de zeldzame steen verkocht en verdween hij spoorloos tot hij in december 2008 weer opdook bij Christie's, waar een Londense juwelier hem voor meer dan $ 24 miljoen kocht.

let's play bonnie and clyde

July 1973, Bay State Antique Automobile Exposition, USA

$175,000

To this day, the story of Bonnie and Clyde continues to inspire filmmakers, musical composers and romance authors, as the wild romance of the outlaw couple has lost none of its fascination through the decades. The car that the outlaw lovers drove in the Thirties, and which they died in a hail of police bullets in 1934, went up for auction in 1973. Even though the old Ford V8 Sedan wasn't exactly in mint condition, given all its dents and bullet holes, one collector still came up with $ 175,000 for the historically valuable vehicle.

L'histoire de Bonnie et Clyde est encore une source d'inspiration pour cinéastes, compositeurs de music-halls et auteurs de romans car le thème de l'idylle échevelée de deux brigands reste d'actualité, au fil des décennies. La voiture à bord de laquelle les amants terribles roulaient dans les années 30 et dans laquelle ils furent tués par une pluie de balles tirées par la police en 1934 fut proposée aux enchères en 1973. Bien que la vieille Ford V8 Sedan, toute cabossée et trouée de balles, ne se présentât pas sous son meilleur jour, un collectionneur déboursa 175 000 dollars pour ce précieux véhicule historique.

Ook vandaag nog inspireert het verhaal van Bonnie en Clyde filmmakers, musicalcomponisten en schrijvers van romantische verhalen. De wilde romance van het bandietenkoppel blijft fascineren, zelfs na al die decennia. De auto waarmee ze in de jaren '30 reden, en waarin ze in 1934 door de politie werden neergekogeld, ging in 1973 onder de hamer. Ook al was de oude Ford V8 berline niet echt in prima staat door alle deuken en kogelgaten, toch legde een verzamelaar $ 175.000 op tafel voor het historisch waardevolle voertuig.

to be as cool as james bond

February 2001, Christie's, London UK

$ 20,487

"Dr. No" is the first James Bond movie ever as well as the prelude to a series of novel-movie versions that continue to write film history to this day. His role as the original Agent 007 made Sean Connery world-famous. His weapon, a Walther Cal. 4-5 LP Model 53 (Air Pistol Non Gun, Promo-Only), which he draws lightning-quick on the bad guys, went up for sale in February 2001 at Christie's, an auction of nostalgic articles, which drew a large number of fans. The man who bought it paid more than $ 20,000.

« James Bond 007 contre Dr. No », le tout premier film de James Bond, est le début d'une série d'adaptations cinématographiques de romans qui marquent aujourd'hui encore l'histoire du cinéma. Le premier agent 007 fut Sean Connery à qui le rôle valut une renommée mondiale. Son arme, un Walther Cal. 4-5 LP Modèle 53 (pistolet à air comprimé à un coup), qu'il dégainait dans le film contre le méchant avec une rapidité fulgurante, fut mise aux enchères en février 2001 lors d'une vente d'objets pour supporters nostalgiques où se pressèrent les visiteurs. L'acheteur déboursa plus de 20 000 dollars.

"Dr. No" is de allereerste James Bond film en de voorloper van een reeks verfilmde romans die ook vandaag nog filmgeschiedenis schrijven. Zijn rol als originele Agent 007 maakte Sean Connery wereldberoemd. Zijn wapen, een Walther Cal. 4-5 LP Model 53 (luchtpistool, enkel voor promodoeleinden), dat hij sneller dan de schurken trekt, werd in februari van 2001 bij Christie's geveild in het kader van een veiling van nostalgische artikelen en het lokte meteen heel wat fans. De uiteindelijke koper betaalde er ruim $ 20.000 voor.

01 ursula, undress!

February 2001, Christie's, London UK

$ 59,755

To emerge from the sea like Honey Ryder in the James Bond thriller "Dr. No" just once—this is what must have been on the minds of the women present at Christie's Auction House in February 2001. Who could forget the first James Bond movie from 1962 in which beautiful Swiss actress Ursula Andress made a serious statement in her bikini? Considered morally questionable before, the two-piece swimsuit became a worldwide fashion hit after the spy thriller. It was a new standard in movie and fashion history that changed ownership in London for a cool $ 59,755.

Émerger des flots telle Honey Ryder dans « James Bond contre Dr. No » – c'est sûrement ce qu'auraient aimé faire les invitées de Christie's, en ce mois de février 2001. Dans ce premier film de James Bond, en 1962, la belle suissesse Ursula Andress posa un véritable jalon avec son bikini : ce maillot de bain deux pièces considéré jusqu'alors comme moralement douteux devint soudain, après ce thriller plein d'agents secrets, un fabuleux succès de mode dans le monde entier. Une pièce innovante de l'histoire culturelle et cinématographique qui trouva un nouveau propriétaire pour la somme rondelette de 59 755 dollars.

Eén keertje uit de zee te voorschijn kunnen komen zoals Honey Ryder het deed in de James Bond thriller "Dr. No" – dat moeten de vrouwen die aanwezig waren in het veilinghuis van Christie's in februari 2001 gedacht hebben. Wie herinnert zich immers de eerste James Bond film uit 1962 niet, waarin de mooie Zwitserse actrice Ursula Andress in haar bikini een serieus statement maakte? Waar het voorheen nog als moreel twijfelachtig beschouwd werd, werd het tweedelige zwempak na de spionthriller een wereldwijde hit. Het was een nieuwe standaard in de film- en modegeschiedenis, die voor een aardige $ 59.755 van eigenaar wisselde.

k.i.t.t. and michael part ways

June 2008, eBay online

$ 53.000

Back in the Eighties, the TV series "Knight Rider" took the ratings by storm, and not without its reasons. For one, it starred suave Michael Knight. And then, of course, it featured K.I.T.T., the innovative computer car with artificial intelligence. This extraordinary set of wheels was based on a thoroughly converted 1982 Pontiac TransAm. Only three of these "K.I.T.T." TransAms were ever built—two of them wound up in museums, while the third one sold for a cool $ 53,000 at an eBay auction.

Dans les années 80, la série « Knight Rider » jouissait, à juste titre, d'une grande popularité : d'une part, il y avait le héros relax Michael Knight. D'autre part, bien sûr, sa voiture K.I.T.T., un véhicule novateur équipé d'un ordinateur de bord doté d'une intelligence artificielle. Pour cette prodigieuse auto, on avait modifié à grands frais une Pontiac Trans Am, année de construction 1982. Dans le monde entier, il n'y en avait que trois exemplaires – dont deux se trouvent aujourd'hui dans des musées américains. La troisième K.I.T.T. atteignit, à une enchère eBay, la coquette somme de 53 000 dollars.

In de jaren tachtig was de TV-serie "Knight Rider" een geweldige kijkcijferhit en niet zonder reden. Zo werd de hoofdrol vertolkt door de beminnelijke Michael Knight. En ... je had natuurlijk K.I.T.T., de innovatieve computerwagen met artificiële intelligentie. Deze buitengewone computer op wielen was gebaseerd op een grondig omgebouwde Pontiac TransAm van 1982. Slechts drie van deze "K.I.T.T." TransAms zijn er ooit gebouwd – twee ervan staan in musea terwijl de derde in een eBay veiling werd verkocht voor een coole $ 53.000.

fight against darth vader

December 2008, Profiles of History, Calabasas Hills USA

$ 240,000

The "Star Wars" episodes by director George Lucas have made movie history—due in no small part to many unique and innovative details. Subsequent Sci-Fi movies have always borrowed from the pioneering ideas that helped define the "Star Wars" movies. Take, for example, the light sabers that offer futuristic duels the good, old swashbuckling way. One of those light sabers, used by Luke Skywalker in "Star Wars: A New Hope" and "The Empire Strikes Back", was auctioned off in late 2008 for a whopping $ 240,000.

Les épisodes de « La Guerre des étoiles », épopée créée par George Lucas, marquèrent l'histoire du cinéma par de nombreuses trouvailles uniques et innovantes. Les films de science-fiction plus récents renferment régulièrement bien des éléments précurseurs qui caractérisent la saga de la Guerre des étoiles. Les sabres lasers par exemple permettent des combats futuristes à la manière des bons vieux héros de cap et d'épée. L'un des sabres lasers que Luke Skywalker emploie dans les épisodes « Un nouvel espoir » et « L'Empire contre-attaque » est parti aux enchères fin 2008 pour la jolie somme de 240 000 dollars.

De "Star Wars"-episodes van regisseur George Lucas hebben filmgeschiedenis geschreven – wat grotendeels te danken is aan de vele unieke en innovatieve details. Latere sciencefictionfilms haalden allemaal hun inspiratie uit de baanbrekende Star Wars-films. Een goed voorbeeld zijn de lichtzwaarden waarmee futuristische duels worden uitgevochten in de stijl van de goede oude zwaardgevechten van vroeger. Een van die lichtzwaarden, dat door Luke Skywalker werd gehanteerd in "Star Wars: A New Hope" en "The Empire Strikes Back", werd eind 2008 geveild voor het duizelingwekkende bedrag van $ 240.000.

© Getty Images

01 worth every penny

May 2007, Cinema-against-AIDS, Cannes FRANCE

$350,000

There are moments in life that money can't buy. Or are there? How about a kiss from, say, George Clooney, one of the sexiest men alive? Priceless? Try again, because that's exactly what was being offered at the charity event Cinema-against-AIDS in Cannes, France. Actually, the lady with the highest bid got two for the price of one: She got a kiss from Hollywood's hottest single, while her affluent husband got to the price for it—a whopping 350,000 bucks.

Il y a des moments dans la vie qui ne s'achètent pas. Si ? Un baiser de George Clooney, l'un des hommes vivants les plus séduisants, par exemple ? Inabordable ? Et bien non. C'est ce qui a été mis aux enchères lors du gala annuel de bienfaisance « Cinéma contre le sida » à Cannes. La dame qui fit l'enchère gagnante est double-ment chanceuse : elle reçut un baiser du célibataire le plus courtisé d'Hollywood et c'est son compagnon fortuné qui s'acquitta des 350 000 dollars.

Er zijn zo van die momenten in het leven die met geen geld ter wereld te koop zijn. Of toch? Wat zou je zeggen van een kus van, pakweg, George Clooney, één van de meest sexy mannen ter wereld? Onbetaalbaar, zeg je? Nou, dat was precies wat te koop werd aangeboden tijdens het liefdadigheidsevenement "Cinema-against-AIDS" in Cannes, Frankrijk. De dame met het hoogste bod had meteen twee keer prijs: ze kreeg een kus van Hollywoods meest begeerde vrijgezel terwijl haar welvarende echtgenoot de prijs mocht betalen: 350.000 dollar, of wat had je gedacht?

the first lady of france—in the buff

April 2008, Christie's, New York USA

© Associated Press

In the 1990s, her pay rate of roughly $ 7.5 million per annum made Carla Bruni one of the best-paid photography models in the world. It was during this time (1993) that she posed for the great black-and-white act photograph that caused a major sensation in April 2008 when it was put up or auction at Christie's. But don't look to Carla Bruni's career as a supermodel or her popular Chanson recordings as the cause for all the hoopla—it was her wedding to the French president, Nicolas Sarkozy, in February 2008 which promptly caused asking prices for the picture to go through the roof.

Dans les années 1990, Carla Bruni, dont les revenus s'élevaient à quelque 7,5 millions de dollars par an, comptait parmi les mannequins les plus connus et les mieux payés au monde. C'est de cette époque (1993) que date le grand nu photographique en noir et blanc dont la mise aux enchères en avril 2008 chez Christie's fit grand bruit. L'agitation n'était due ni à la carrière de mannequin à succès de Carla Bruni ni à ses disques populaires mais à son mariage en février 2008 avec le président français Nicolas Sarkozy, qui fit grimper en flèche le prix de la photo.

In de jaren 1990 maakte haar gage van grofweg $ 7,5 miljoen per jaar Carla Bruni één van de best betaalde fotomodellen ter wereld. Het was in die periode (1993) dat ze poseerde voor de grote zwart-witfoto die zoveel ophef veroorzaakte toen hij in april 2008 bij Christie's onder de hamer ging. Het was echter niet Carla Bruni's carrière als supermodel of haar populaire chansonalbums die voor alle opschudding zorgde – dat was haar huwelijk in februari 2008 met de Franse president, Nicolas Sarkozy. Hierdoor swingde de vraagprijs voor de foto meteen de pan uit.

cher's black little nothing

October 2006, Julien's, West Hollywood USA

© Getty Images

$60,000

Cher's song "If I could turn back time" was a huge success, went gold in the U.K. and even platinum in the U.S. But, more than the song itself, what really caught everybody's attention was Cher's outfit: A black veil consisting of nothing but a net cat suit and a tight body caused serious controversy in 1989. Music stations like MTV consequently banned the video version of her song to late-night TV. In 2006 her hot outfit suddenly celebrated its comeback—when sold for $ 60,000 at an auction.

La chanson de Cher « If I could turn back time », hit planétaire, fut disque d'or en Grande-Bretagne et disque de platine aux Etats-Unis. Mais plus que la chanson, c'est le costume de scène de l'artiste qui attira l'attention. Sa tenue ultra légère, composée d'un body transparent et d'un combiné-slip échancré, fit l'objet de vives critiques en 1989. Les chaînes musicales, comme MTV, reléguèrent le clip dans les programmes de fin de soirée. Cette tenue sexy fit son retour en 2006 – et fut adjugée lors d'une vente aux enchères pour 60 000 dollars.

Chers song "If I could turn back time" was een enorm succes, veroverde goud in het Verenigd Koninkrijk en zelfs platina in de VS. Maar, meer nog dan de song zelf was het Chers outfit die ieders aandacht trok: een zwarte sluier louter bestaande uit een niets verhullende bodystocking en een strakke body veroorzaakte toen in 1989 heel wat controverse. Muziekzenders zoals MTV verbanden de videoversie van haar song naar de late avond. In 2006 vierde haar outfit plots een sensationele comeback toen deze tijdens een veiling voor $ 60.000 werd verkocht.

che guevara's revolutionary bangs

October 2007, Heritage, Dallas USA

When Heritage Auctions sold a strand of hair from Che Guevara in Dallas, Texas, in October 1967, it caused quite a stir. Even in the run-up, the auction house received numerous threats, creating the need for beefed-up security during the auction itself. The strand of hair from the Cuban politician, revolutionary and guerilla leader ultimately went to a 61-year-old man from Rosenberg near Houston, who intended to add Che's bangs as yet another interesting item to his vast collection of 1960's memorabilia.

La mise aux enchères, en octobre 1967, par Heritage Auctions à Dallas, Texas, d'une mèche de cheveux de Che Guevara déclencha une grande agitation. Avant l'événement, la maison de ventes aux enchères reçut des menaces et pendant les enchères, elle fut sous la protection d'une équipe de sécurité renforcée. C'est finalement un homme de 61 ans, originaire de Rosenberg, Houston, qui fit l'acquisition des cheveux du politicien, révolutionnaire et chef de guérilla cubain. Avec la mèche du Che, il souhaitait apporter à sa collection d'objets des années 1960 cette pièce intéressante.

Toen Heritage Auctions in oktober 1967 in Dallas, Texas, een streng haar van Che Guevara verkocht, veroorzaakte dit nogal wat deining. Al in de aanloop ontving het veilinghuis talrijke bedreigingen zodat er voor de veiling zelf strenge veiligheidsmaatregelen werden genomen. De streng haar van de Cubaanse politicus, revolutionair en guerillaleider ging uiteindelijk naar een 61-jarige man uit Rosenberg nabij Houston, die Che's pony als interessante aanwinst bij zijn al uitgebreide collectie van jaren '60-memorabilia wilde voegen.

contents

rich and beautiful   01

happy birthday, mr. president // a little piece of cloth with plenty sex appeal // jimi hendrix as up close as it gets //
the white album no. 0000005 // what a scary passport // holiday with mr. bean // here to save the world //
elvis presley's peacock outfit // a guide to marilyn's companions // join the sgt. pepper's lonely hearts club band //
dress up for a breakfast at tiffany's // no new queen for marie antoinette's pearls // the wittelsbach diamond //
let's play bonnie and clyde // to be as cool as james bond // ursula, undress! // k.i.t.t. and michael part ways //
fight against darth vader // worth every penny // the first lady of france—in the buff // cher's black little nothing //
che guevara's revolutionary bangs

expensive   02

a true classic—the bugatti royale // double eagle—the most expensive coin // allah's words of immeasurable value //
the violin of the devil's fiddler // the most expensive fossil // the magic price for words // the most expensive scrabble board
// what time is it? // the most expensive baseball card // a very personal declaration of independence //
the first adventure of spiderman // sex.com for millions of dollars // a very special license plate // 5 £ + auction = $ 31,200 //
the most expensive bottle of wine // white truffles—edible gold // andy warhol meets velvet underground //
pablo picasso's masterpiece // the world's most expensive cow // the most expensive stamp ever

curiosities   03

my holy toast // the beautiful teeth of paris hilton // there's money in cornflakes // chocolate from the south pole //
britney's real gum back // a royal piece of cake // royal stockings from way back when // not tonight, josephine //
what nobody needs // the luckiest phone number ever: 8x8 // what a good old beer // beam me up, scotty! //
make love not war // a kid named erich honecker // adolf hitler's globe // look into the future with nostradamus //
it's magic: houdini's water torture cell // buying drugs from the government // katie's top model hairstyle //
a "holy" car—the pope's vw golf // one key could have saved them all // whole life for sale

locations   04

my home is my prison // the wall must go // room for a real mega party // my home, my car, my hamlet //
how big: galaxy for sale // the minsk—a giant of the seven seas // be a part of disneyland—on a tombstone //
a window that changed world history // stairway to heaven // anybody want to buy belgium? // big wheel keeps on turning //
your name on mount mckinley // the sexiest millennium party ever

a true classic—the bugatti royale

November 1987, Christie's, London UK

$ 8,700,000

Among experts, the Bugatti Type 41 is simply known as the "Bugatti Royale". The luxury automobile made its debut in the public at Germany's Nürburgring in June 1928. With 250 horsepower, a 190-liter fuel tank, a top speed of 200 KPH and a raised elephant as its hood ornament, the Bugatti quickly became a household name among the wealthy. Even so, its expensive materials and costly production allowed only six units to be produced, all of which still exist today. One of these rare automobiles sold at an auction in November 1987 for almost 9 million dollars.

Les connaisseurs appellent la Bugatti Type 41 tout simplement « Bugatti Royale ». Cette luxueuse automobile fut présentée au public pour la première fois en juin 1928 sur le Nürburgring. Avec une puissance de 250 ch, un réservoir à essence de 190 litres, une vitesse de pointe de 200 km/h et un bouchon de radiateur figurant un éléphant dressé sur ses pattes de derrière, la Bugatti se fit rapidement un nom au sein de l'élite de la planète. Etant donné la cherté des matériaux et les coûts de production élevés, seules six voitures furent construites. Les six exemplaires existent encore aujourd'hui. L'une de ces raretés fut adjugée en novembre 1987 pour presque 9 millions de dollars.

Onder experts staat de Bugatti Type 41 gewoonweg bekend als de "Bugatti Royale". Deze luxeauto maakte zijn debuut op de Duitse Nürburgring in juni 1928. Met zijn 250 pk, benzinetank van 190 liter, topsnelheid van 200 km/u en de staande olifant als motorkapversiering raakte de Bugatti al snel ingeburgerd bij de rijken. Maar door de kostbare materialen en dure productie konden amper zes stuks worden geproduceerd, die allemaal nog bestaan. Een van deze zeldzame auto's werd in november van 1987 geveild voor bijna 9 miljoen dollar.

double eagle—the most expensive coin

July 2002, Sotheby's, New York USA

$ 7,600,000

© Associated Press

One result of the California Gold Rush of 1849 was the introduction of the double version of the 10-dollar "Eagle" coin in use since 1795. This was the gold coin called the "Double Eagle" with a value of 20 dollars. Redesigned in 1907, the coin continued to be minted until 1933. Owing to the world financial crisis, all "Double Eagles" of that year were melted—except for one. That makes the Double Eagle from 1933 the most valuable coin in the world today, since it's the only one remaining. The last time it was auctioned off was in July 2002 at Sotheby's in New York, where it sold for $ 7,600,000.

En raison de la ruée vers l'or en Californie, fut introduit en 1849 le pendant à l'Aigle d'or de 10 dollars usité depuis 1795 : le Double Aigle d'or, une pièce en or d'une valeur de 20 dollars. Redessinée en 1907, la pièce fut frappée jusqu'en 1933. À cause de la Grande Dépression, les monnaies du dernier millésime furent détruites – c'est ainsi que le Double Aigle d'or de 1933 est devenu la pièce la plus précieuse au monde car il n'en reste qu'une seule. Sa dernière vente aux enchères remonte à 2002 chez Sotheby's à New York où elle atteignit le prix record pour une monnaie de collection : 7 600 000 dollars.

Eén gevolg van de Californische Goudkoorts in 1849 was de invoering van de dubbele versie van de "Eagle" van 10 dollar die sinds 1795 werd gebruikt. Het ging om de gouden munt met een waarde van 20 dollar, de zogenaamde "Double Eagle". De munt, die in 1907 werd hertekend, bleef tot in 1933 in omloop. Omwille van de wereldwijde financiële crisis werden alle "Double Eagles" van dat jaar gesmolten – op één na. De Double Eagle uit 1933 is vandaag dan ook de waardevolste munt ter wereld omdat het de laatste in zijn soort is. De vorige keer dat hij werd geveild, in juli van 2002 bij Sotheby's in New York, ging hij voor $ 7.600.000 van de hand.

allah's words of immeasurable value

November 2007, Christie's, London UK

$ 1,600,000

© Fotolia, Smrtnick

To any faithful Muslim, the Koran presents a highly valuable book in and of itself. In November 2007, a very special edition of the Holy Book of Islam came up for auction: A Koran dating back to 1203 A.D., whose writing has been perfectly preserved. The verses in it were written in gold and the signature of their writer, Yahya Ibn Muhammad Ibn 'Umar, is clearly visible. This valuable artifact of art and religious history went on sale for a proud $ 1.6 million. The acceptance of bid went to a British art dealer, who stated his intent to resell the book in the Orient.

Pour tout musulman croyant, le Coran en soi est un livre de grande valeur. En novembre 2007, une édition tout à fait spéciale du livre sacré de l'islam est tombée sous le marteau : un Coran, daté de 1203 ap. J.C. dont le texte est entièrement conservé. Les versets sont écrits en lettres d'or et distinctement signés par leur rédacteur Yahya Ibn Muhammad Ibn 'Umar. Cette pièce précieuse pour l'histoire de l'art et des religions put être vendue pour la somme considérable de 1,6 million de dollars. L'adjudication alla à un marchand d'objets d'art anglais qui indiqua vouloir revendre le livre en Orient.

Voor iedere gelovige moslim is de Koran op zich al een erg waardevol boek. In november van 2007 ging een zeer bijzondere uitgave van het Heilige Boek van de Islam onder de hamer: een Koran uit het jaar 1203, met een perfect bewaard schrift. De verzen zijn in goud geschreven en de handtekening van de auteur, Yahya Ibn Muhammad Ibn 'Umar, is duidelijk leesbaar. Dit waardevolle kunstwerk en religieuze boek werd voor de mooie som van $ 1,6 miljoen verkocht. Het bod kwam van een Britse kunsthandelaar, die aangaf het boek in het Oosten te gaan verkopen.

the violin of the devil's fiddler

November 2005, Sotheby's, London UK

$1,000,000

Carlo Bergonzi as well as Antonio Stradivari, Guiseppe Antonio Guarneri und Nicola Amati are among the most influential violin builders of Italy. The rare and sometimes wrong use of brand names makes his violins difficult to find, except for enthusiasts who highly appreciate them for their first-rate quality and their fascinating sound. One of these rare instruments belonged to virtuoso Niccolò Paganini, who used to hold all of Europe spellbound with his violin play in the early 19th Century. In June 2006, this fine instrument sold for $ 1,000,000 at an auction.

Carlo Bergonzi est, avec Antonio Stradivari, Giuseppe Antonio Guarneri et Nicola Amati, un des plus grands luthiers italiens. Les rares violons portant son étiquette – quand celle-ci n'est pas falsifiée – sont difficiles à trouver. D'une qualité exceptionnelle, ils possèdent une sonorité fascinante que les musiciens aiment par-dessus tout. Un de ces rares violons appartint jadis au virtuose Niccolò Paganini qui enthousiasma l'Europe entière au début du 19ème siècle avec son jeu fabuleux. Cet admirable instrument fut vendu aux enchères en juin 2006 pour la somme considérable d'un million de dollars.

Carlo Bergonzi is samen met Antonio Stradivari, Giuseppe Antonio Guarneri en Nicola Amati een van de invloedrijkste vioolbouwers van Italië. Het zeldzame en vaak verkeerde gebruik van merknamen maakt dat zijn violen moeilijk te vinden zijn, behalve voor de liefhebbers die de topkwaliteit en het fascinerende geluid ervan op prijs stellen. Een van die zeldzame instrumenten behoorde toe aan virtuoos Niccolò Paganini, die in het begin van de 19de eeuw heel Europa in de ban hield met zijn vioolspel. In juni van 2006 werd dit geraffineerde instrument op een veiling verkocht voor het aanzienlijke bedrag van $ 1 miljoen.

the most expensive fossil

October 1997, Sotheby's, New York USA

$ 8,360,000

The most complete Tyrannosaurus Rex ever found was given the adorable name "Sue" by its discoverers. Sue died around 65 million years ago. A grave of sediments and water, which compounded into rock through all the years, held her until the year 1990 when paleontologists uncovered the well-preserved skeleton of the dinosaur lady. Following extensive analyses, her bones were put up for auction at Sotheby's in 1997, to be purchased by the Field Museum of Natural History of Chicago for the gigantic price of over $ 8 million.

Le Tyrannosaurus rex le plus complet jamais trouvé fut surnommé « Sue » par les paléontologues qui le découvrirent. Sue mourut il y a 65 millions d'années. Elle reposait dans sa tombe, composée de sédiments et d'eau pétrifiés au fil du temps, jusqu'à ce qu'en 1990 une équipe de paléontologues mette au jour le squelette bien conservé de cette femelle dinosaure. Après des observations scientifiques approfondies, ses os furent vendus aux enchères en 1997 chez Sotheby's et le Field Museum of Natural History de Chicago se porta acquéreur pour un prix astronomique dépassant 8 millions de dollars.

De meest complete Tyrannosaurus Rex die ooit werd gevonden, werd door de ontdekkers ervan "Sue" gedoopt. Sue stierf zo'n 65 miljoen jaar geleden en lag in een graf van sediment en water, dat door de jaren heen tot steen was samengedrukt, tot paleontologen het goed bewaarde skelet van het dinosaurusvrouwtje in 1990 opgroeven. Na uitgebreide analyses werden de beenderen in 1997 geveild bij Sotheby's en gekocht door het Field Museum of Natural History (Natuurhistorisch Museum) van Chicago voor de gigantische prijs van ruim $ 8 miljoen.

the magic price of words

December 2007, Sotheby's, London UK

$3,985,410

© Associated Press

"The Tales of Beedle the Bard" is the title of a book by Harry-Potter author J.K. Rowling. She didn't write it by hand and provide it with amiable illustrations just to tell beautiful stories, though—she also created her fairy tale book for a charitable purpose: All profits from the sale of her fascinating and artistic book go to "The Children's Voice"—a project for the benefit of disadvantaged children. So it's only fitting for the original manuscript to be auctioned off at almost $ 4 million.

« Les Contes de Beedle le Barde » est un livre de la romancière J. K. Rowling, auteur d'Harry Potter. La romancière ne rédigea pas ce livre, manuscrit et illustré avec amour, uniquement pour raconter de belles histoires – elle créa ce conte pour enfants pour une œuvre de bienfaisance : l'argent récolté avec ce merveilleux livre artistiquement décoré revient intégralement à « The Children's Voice » – un projet mené par une œuvre de charité au profit d'enfants défavorisés. C'est donc une bonne chose que le manuscrit original ait rapporté aux enchères presque 4 millions de dollars.

"The Tales of Beedle the Bard" is de titel van een boek van J.K. Rowling, de schrijfster van de Harry Potter boeken. Ze schreef het met de hand en versierde het met prachtige illustraties, niet alleen maar om een mooi verhaal te vertellen – ze maakte haar sprookjesboek voor een liefdadigheidsproject: alle opbrengsten uit de verkoop van haar fascinerende en artistieke boek gaan naar "The Children's Voice" – een project ten voordele van kansarme kinderen. Het is dan ook een goede zaak dat het originele manuscript voor bijna $ 4 miljoen werd geveild.

02 the most expensive scrabble board

October 2008, eBay online

$ 30,000

Scrabble isn't just any popular game for evening entertainment—no, even stars like Mel Gibson or Keanu Reeves and Queen Elizabeth II love the game with the alphabet. To this end, the perfect accessory for celebrity Scrabble comes from Hasbro and the House of Swarovski: A Scrabble board made of glass with 30,000 original Swarovski crystals. The glittering luxury game has been known to fetch as much as $ 30,000 during a charity eBay auction—not exactly a cheap way to play the game!

Le scrabble n'est pas qu'un jeu de société pour soirées conviviales – non, des célébrités telles que Mel Gibson ou Keanu Reeves et la reine Elisabeth II aiment aussi ce jeu de lettres. L'accessoire adéquat pour ce club sélect est issu de la maison Swarovski : c'est une planche de jeu de scrabble en verre garni de 30 000 véritables cristaux Swarovski. Le scintillant et luxueux jeu produit par le fabricant de cristal autrichien coûtait déjà plus de 30 000 dollars sur eBay – le plaisir du jeu n'est pas toujours bon marché !

Scrabble is niet zomaar een populair bordspel voor 's avonds – nee, zelfs sterren als Mel Gibson of Keanu Reeves en Koningin Elizabeth II spelen graag het letterspel. Het perfecte scrabbleaccessoire voor celebrities komt dan ook van Hasbro en het huis Swarovski: een glazen scrabblebord met 30.000 originele Swarovski-kristallen. Tijdens een veiling op eBay ging het schitterende luxespel voor maar liefst $ 30.000 van de hand – niet bepaald een goedkope manier van spelen!

what time is it?

December 1999, Sotheby's, New York USA

$11,000,000

© Fotolia, Chushkin

Swiss watch manufacturer Patek Philippe has been famous for its extraordinary, exclusive and highly precise watches since the mid-19th Century. One of its most intricate pieces is the "Henry Graves Super-complication" from the year 1933. This extraordinary pocket watch comes with an amazing 24 additional functions, consists of 900 parts and is made of 18 Karat gold. The unique piece, exclusively made for a New York banker, Mr. Henry Graves, Jr., fetched more than $ 11 million at an auction at Sotheby's.

La manufacture horlogère suisse Patek Philippe est réputée depuis la seconde moitié du 19ème siècle pour ses montres de haute précision, extraordinaires et exclusives. L'une de ses pièces les plus raffinées est la « montre à complication Henry Graves » réalisée en 1933. Cette montre de poche exceptionnelle, do-tée de 24 complications, composée de 900 pièces en tout, est en or 18 carats. Cette pièce unique réalisée à la demande d'un banquier new-yorkais, Mr. Henry Graves Jr., fut adjugée lors d'une vente aux enchères chez Sotheby's pour plus de 11 millions de dollars.

Sinds het midden van de 19de eeuw staat de Zwitserse horlogemaker Patek Philippe bekend voor zijn buitengewone, exclusieve en uiterst precieze uurwerken. Een van die precisie-uurwerken is de "Henry Graves Supercomplication" uit 1933. Dit buitengewone zakhorloge heeft maar liefst 24 functies, telt 900 onderdelen en bestaat uit 18-karaatsgoud. Het unieke stuk, dat speciaal voor de New Yorkse bankier Henry Graves, Jr. werd gemaakt, ging voor meer dan $ 11 miljoen van de hand op een veiling bij Sotheby's.

$2,800,000

The T206 Honus Wagner baseball card from 1909 is considered the "Holy Grail" or "Mona Lisa" among collectors of baseball cards. It is estimated that only 60 of them were ever made. The card depicts none other than Honus Wagner, the famous shortstop for the Pittsburgh Pirates from 1897 to 1917. It was his legendary speed that earned him the nickname "Flying Dutchman". Very well preserved by September 2007, one T206 sold for the record sum of $ 2.8 million.

La carte de baseball T206 Honus Wagner de 1909 est une sorte de « Saint Graal » ou « La Joconde » des cartes de collection. On suppose qu'il n'en existe pas plus de 60 exemplaires. Elle représente la star du baseball américain Honus Wagner qui joua de 1897 à 1917 pour les Pirates de Pittsburgh. Sa rapidité légendaire lui valut le surnom de « Hollandais volant ». En septembre 2007, cette carte de collection très bien conservée fut vendue aux enchères pour la somme record de 2,8 millions de dollars.

Het T206 Honus Wagner honkbalkaartje uit 1909 wordt door verzamelaars van honkbalkaartjes als de "Heilige Graal" of de "Mona Lisa" beschouwd. Men schat dat er amper 60 van werden gemaakt. Het kaartje toont niemand anders dan Honus Wagner, de beroemde shortstop van de Pittsburgh Pirates van 1897 tot 1917. Zijn legendarische snelheid leverde hem de bijnaam "Flying Dutchman" op. Een T206-kaartje, dat in september van 2007 nog goed bewaard was gebleven, werd voor een recordbedrag van $ 2,8 miljoen verkocht.

WAGNER, PITTSBURG

© Fotolia, Carsten Reisinger

$17,400,000

The American War for Independence, which gave the 13 British colonies in North America the rights of an independent nation and which led to the formation of the United States of America, is quite possibly one of the politically most influential wars of the last millennium. Collectors deeply value rare memorabilia from this important era. In June 2006, that was exactly what came up for auction at Sotheby's in New York. It involved four striped flags—only 30 of which are still known to exist worldwide. For that reason, the highest bidder paid $ 17,400,000 for all four flags.

La guerre d'indépendance américaine qui permit à 13 colonies britanniques d'Amérique du nord d'accéder à l'autonomie et conduisit à la naissance des Etats-Unis d'Amérique est peut-être l'une des guerres du dernier millénaire dont la portée politique fut la plus importante. Les collectionneurs sont à l'affût des rares souvenirs de cette époque décisive. En juin 2006, la maison de ventes Sotheby's de New York en vendit quelques uns aux enchères : 4 drapeaux à rayures dont il n'existe plus que 30 spécimens dans le monde. Les quatre drapeaux trouvèrent donc preneur pour plus de 17 millions de dollars.

De Amerikaanse Onafhankelijkheidsoorlog is op politiek vlak misschien wel een van de meest invloedrijke oorlogen van het voorbije millennium. Hierdoor kregen de 13 Britse kolonies in Noord-Amerika immers de rechten van een onafhankelijk land kregen en deze oorlog leidde uiteindelijk tot de geboorte van de Verenigde Staten van Amerika. Verzamelaars hebben heel wat over voor zeldzame memorabilia uit die belangrijke periode. In juni 2006 werden ze op hun wenken bediend: bij Sotheby's in New York werden vier gestreepte vlaggen geveild – waarvan er over heel de wereld maar 30 meer bestaan. De hoogste bieder betaalde dan ook bovenaan 17 miljoen voor de vier vlaggen.

02

the first adventure of spiderman

October 2007, ComicLink, New York USA

$ 227,000

"Amazing Fantasy #15" of Marvel Comics from 1962 gives rise to a major comic hero of the 20th Century—Spiderman. The superhero with the powers of a spider makes the August issue of this comic series very special, indeed. Even though copies of that issue still exist in sufficient numbers, very few of them are preserved well enough to be rated 9.4 or "near-mint condition". In October 2007, one of those copies was put up for auction for the enthusiast price of no less than $ 227,000.

Le numéro 15 du magazine Amazing Fantasy édité par Marvel Comics voit la naissance en 1962 d'un héros de bande dessinée qui sera très populaire au 20ème siècle : Spider-Man. Avec le super-héros aux propriétés d'araignée, l'édition du magazine d'août de cette année-là devint alors un numéro très particulier. Et bien qu'il en reste quelques spécimens, les exemplaires bien conservés portant la note 9.4 ou « near-mint-condition » (presque à l'état neuf) sont rares. Une de ces raretés très convoitées fut vendue aux enchères en octobre 2007 et cédée à un prix de collectionneur de quelque 227 000 dollars.

"Amazing Fantasy #15" van Marvel Comics uit 1962 betekende het begin van een belangrijke stripheld uit de 20ste eeuw: Spiderman. De superheld met de eigenschappen van een spin maakt van het augustusnummer van deze strip een heel speciale uitgave. Ook al zijn er nog genoeg exemplaren van dat nummer, toch zijn er maar weinig goed genoeg bewaard gebleven om een 9,4 of "near-mint condition" (bijna perfecte staat) te halen. In oktober van 2007 werd een van die exemplaren geveild; een fan betaalde er niet minder dan $ 227.000 voor.

sex.com for millions of dollars

January 2005, private, USA

$12,000,000

© Fotolia, manolito

The most frequently searched term on the Internet is "sex", and the domain "www.sex.com" records more than 25 million clicks every day. That makes this website a moneymaking machine in the truest sense— and in January 2005, it was priced to sell accordingly: $ 12 million is what the new owner paid for the user rights to the domain. Does that new owner use sex. com to fill it with the expected contents or for different purpose? Well, all it takes is one mouse click to find out ...

Sur Internet, le mot-clé le plus recherché est « sexe ». Et le domaine « www.sex.com » compte quotidiennement plus de 25 millions de clics. Ce site Internet est donc littéralement l'équivalent d'une planche à billets – et son prix de vente en janvier 2005 fut logiquement à la hauteur : le nouveau propriétaire a versé 12 millions de dollars pour la jouissance du domaine. Pour savoir si le nouveau propriétaire a mis sur sex. com les contenus implicites ou s'il a opté pour une autre utilisation, il suffit de cliquer ...

De vaakst opgezochte term op internet is "seks" en de domeinnaam "www.sex.com" wordt elke dag meer dan 25 miljoen keer aangeklikt. Dat maakt van deze website een winstgevende zaak in de ware betekenis van het woord en het prijskaartje in januari van 2005 was er dan ook naar: de nieuwe eigenaar betaalde $ 12 miljoen voor de gebruiksrechten op de domeinnaam. Vult de nieuwe eigenaar sex.com met de verwachte inhoud, of met andere dingen? Daar kom je zo achter met een muisklik...

$ 366,845

© Fotolia, Tub

Many people like the idea of having their initials on their license plates. But how much would they be willing to pay for it? Rob Harverson of Great Britain, who already has 10 other vanity tags, laid down more than $ 350,000 for his license plate "1RH" at an auction. The widely publicized event for vanity license plates even produced further highly personalized license combinations at high prices—although none of them topped the sales value of "1RH".

De nombreux conducteurs aiment avoir leurs propres initiales sur la plaque d'immatriculation de leur voiture. Mais combien sont-ils prêts à investir pour ce privilège ? En Grande-Bretagne, Rob Harverson, qui possède déjà une dizaine d'autres numéros d'immatriculation spéciaux, a remporté aux enchères pour plus de 350 000 dollars le numéro 1RH. Lors de cette vente aux enchères de grande envergure dédiée aux immatriculations de voiture, d'autres combinaisons spéciales chèrement mises à prix furent également adjugées – mais aucune ne put dépasser le numéro 1RH.

Veel mensen willen graag hun initialen op hun nummerplaat zien staan. Maar hoeveel hebben ze daar voor over? Rob Harverson uit Groot-Brittannië, die al 10 andere "ijdeltuitplaten" heeft, legde bij een veiling ruim $ 350.000 op tafel voor zijn "1RH". Tijdens dit mediagenieke evenement voor gepersonaliseerde nummerplaten gingen nog meer van dergelijke combinaties voor een stevige prijs van de hand – al kwam geen enkele in de buurt van de prijs die voor "1RH" werd betaald.

$ 31,200

"White Fivers" are 5-£ bank notes printed on white paper by a number of branches of the Bank of England in the 19th Century. Many of these notes remain in good shape today—except for those of the Portsmouth branch. Of the many thousands of "White Fivers" printed there, only six remain today. One of these rare notes was put for auction at Bonham's in London in April 2003. The highest bidder paid $ 31,200 for the bank note originally worth only 5 pounds.

Les « White Fivers » sont des billets de banque de 5 £ sur fond blanc, émis au 19ème siècle par quelques filiales de la Banque d'Angleterre. Plusieurs de ces billets sont encore bien conservés – sauf ceux de la filiale de Portsmouth. Sur les milliers de « White Fivers » qu'elle imprima, seuls six spécimens entiers ont survécu. L'un de ses rares exemplaires fut vendu aux enchères par Bonhams à Londres en avril 2003. Le meilleur enchérisseur remporta pour 31 200 dollars un billet de banque qui ne valait à l'origine que 5 livres.

"White Fivers" zijn bankbiljetten van 5 £ die in de 19de eeuw op wit papier werden gedrukt door enkele kantoren van de Bank van Engeland. Veel van die biljetten zijn vandaag nog in goede staat – behalve die van het kantoor te Portsmouth. Van de duizenden "White Fivers" die daar werden gedrukt, blijven er maar zes meer over. Een van die zeldzame biljetten werd in april van 2003 geveild bij Bonham's in Londen. De hoogste bieder betaalde $ 31.200 voor het bankbiljet dat oorspronkelijk amper 5 pond waard was.

© Getty Images

02 the most expensive bottle of wine

December 1986, Christie's, London UK

$156,450

© Associated Press

What's a few more dollars when it comes to good wine! For example, what may be the last bottle of Château Lafite from 1787. During one spectacular auction at Christie's, Christopher Forbes outbid the publisher of Wine Spectator, Marvin Shanken, to receive acceptance of his bid of more than $ 150,000. Ever since, the most expensive bottle of wine of all times from the world-famous, prestigious vineyard of Château Lafite-Rothschild has been stored at Forbes House on New York's 5th Avenue.

Pour une bonne bouteille de vin, on peut facilement dépenser quelques dollars de plus ! Par exemple, pour ce qui est peut-être la dernière bouteille de Château Lafite datée de 1787. Lors d'une enchère spectaculaire organisée par la traditionnelle maison Christie's, Christopher Forbes surenchérit sur Marvin Shanken, l'éditeur de la revue Wine Spectator et remporta finalement la mise pour plus de 150 000 dollars. La bouteille de vin la plus chère de tous les temps du vénérable et célébrissime domaine Château Lafite-Rothschild repose désormais dans la résidence de Forbes sur la 5ème avenue à New York.

Wat betekenen nu een paar dollars als het om goede wijn gaat! Bijvoorbeeld voor wat misschien wel de laatste fles Château Lafite uit 1787 is. Tijdens een spectaculaire veiling bij Christie's overtroefde Christopher Forbes Marvin Shanken, de uitgever van Wine Spectator, met een bod van ruim $ 150.000. Sindsdien wordt de duurste fles ooit, afkomstig van de wereldberoemde, prestigieuze wijngaard Château Lafite-Rothschild, bewaard in het Forbes House aan 5th Avenue in New York.

white truffle—edible gold

November 2006, Annual World Alba White Truffle Auction, Grinzane ITALY

White truffles are a delicacy as fine as they are rare. The exquisite mushrooms—attempts at growing them remain unsuccessful—can only be stored for two to seven days and only grow naturally in a few regions on Earth. Hence, the odds of finding a number of large specimens are akin to winning the lottery. However, that's exactly what happened near the Italian town of Alba in November 2006, allowing three specimens with a combined weight of 1.5 kilograms to be put for auction. A gourmet out of Hong Kong received the acceptance of bid by offering $ 160,406. All we can say is—bon appetit!

La truffe blanche est un mets aussi rare qu'exquis. Ce noble tubercule que l'on n'est pas encore parvenu à cultiver ne se conserve que de deux à sept jours et ne pousse que dans quelques régions de par le monde – en trouver plusieurs gros spécimens revient donc à décrocher le gros lot. C'est ce qui est arrivé à Alba, en Italie, où trois truffes pesant en tout 1,5 kg furent vendues aux enchères en novembre 2006. Un gourmet de Hong Kong fit l'enchère gagnante pour la somme de 160 406 dollars. Souhaitons-lui bon appétit !

Witte truffels zijn een geraffineerde en zeldzame delicatesse. Deze exquise paddenstoelen – men is er nog altijd niet in geslaagd om ze te kweken – zijn maar twee à zeven dagen lang te bewaren en zijn enkel in een paar streken in de natuur te vinden. De kans om enkele grote exemplaren te vinden, is dus al even groot als de kans om de lotto te winnen. Dat is echter precies wat er in november van 2006 gebeurde in de buurt van het Italiaanse stadje Alba; het resultaat was dat drie exemplaren met een totaal gewicht van 1,5 kilogram konden worden geveild. Het bod van $ 160.406 van een fijnproever uit Hongkong werd aanvaard. Al wat we kunnen zeggen is … smakelijk!

andy warhol meets velvet underground

November 2004, eBay online

$ 155,401

© Fotolia, Andrey Semenov

The legendary "Banana Album" by The Velvet Underground and Nico is a wonderful album to spotlight the wild, late Sixties in New York. First, because of its one-of-a-kind Hippie-Punk music, secondly, because of its cover design featuring the famous Banana by Andy Warhol. Collector Warren Hill of Montreal, Canada, came across a very special edition of the album at a street flea market in New York and bought it for 75 cents. Since it was the limited original edition on which the banana can be peeled, he was then able to sell it for over $ 150,000 on eBay.

Le légendaire album à la banane du groupe The Velvet Underground and Nico est un magnifique morceau de bravoure de la fin délirante des années 60 à New York. D'une part pour la musique inouïe hippie-punk, d'autre part pour la pochette du disque avec la célèbre banane dessinée par Andy Warhol. Le collectionneur Warren Hill de Montréal au Canada découvrit un exemplaire spécial de l'album sur un marché aux puces à New York et l'acheta pour 75 cents. Il put vendre aux enchères sur eBay cette édition originale à tirage limité avec la banane pelée pour plus de 150 000 dollars.

Het legendarische "Banana Album" van The Velvet Underground en Nico is een prachtalbum dat de wilde periode van eind jaren '60 in New York illustreert. Ten eerste door de unieke hippie/punkstijl van de muziek en ten tweede omdat op de hoes de beroemde Banana van Andy Warhol te zien is. Verzamelaar Warren Hill uit het Canadese Montreal vond een heel bijzondere uitgave van het album op een vlooienmarkt in New York en kocht die voor 75 cent. Omdat het om de originele limited edition ging waarvan de banaan kan worden gepeld, kon hij hem voor meer dan $ 150.000 verkopen op eBay.

© Getty Images

pablo picasso's masterpiece

May 2004, Sotheby's, New York USA

SOTHEBY'S

Lot Number: 7

USD ($)	93,000,000
EUR (€)	76,632,000
UK (£)	51,894,000
SWI (F)	118,575,000
JPN (¥)	10,099,800,000

$104,000,000

© Associated Press

Pablo Picasso has created many priceless works of art, but the fact that one of them in particular would sell for a sensational top price at an auction surprised even the most dedicated art experts. "Boy with Pipe" is a painting from 1905, the year that marks Picasso's Rose Period, which makes it a rather untypical painting for the great Spanish graphic artist, painter and sculptor. That, however, did not prevent one aficionado from offering the record sum of $ 104 million.

Pablo Picasso a réalisé de nombreux chefs d'œuvre de grande valeur. Mais que celui-ci justement atteigne aux enchères un prix démentiel a surpris les experts les plus chevronnés : le « Garçon à la pipe » est un tableau peint en 1905 qui marque le début de la période rose de Picasso. C'est donc un tableau plutôt atypique du grand graphiste, peintre et sculpteur espagnol. Un amateur d'art en fit pourtant l'acquisition pour une enchère record de plus de 104 millions de dollars.

Pablo Picasso maakte tal van onschatbare kunstwerken, maar het feit dat één daarvan voor een sensationele prijs werd geveild, verbaasde zelfs de meest gedreven kunstexperts. "Jongen met Pijp" is een schilderij uit 1905, het jaar van de Roze Periode van Picasso. Daarom is het een eerder atypisch schilderij voor deze grootse Spaanse grafische vormgever, schilder en beeldhouwer. Dat weerhield een liefhebber er niet van om het recordbedrag van $ 104 miljoen te bieden.

the world's most expensive cow

September 2008, Sotheby's, London UK

$14,660,000

© Getty Images

A tiger shark in formaldehyde, a sheep preserved the same way, or a diamond-encrusted skull—his objects of art have made Damian Hirst a hotly discussed shock artist since the late Eighties. In Fall 2008, he made headlines again in the form of an auction solely dedicated to selling his works of art. One of its highlights was "The Golden Calf"—a young bull preserved in formaldehyde and partially adorned with gold. It sold for more than $ 14 million.

Un requin tigre dans du formol, un mouton naturalisé ou la réplique d'un crâne d'homme incrusté de diamants – depuis la fin des années quatre-vingts, ses objets d'art font de Damian Hirst un artiste à scandale qui suscite de vives controverses. À l'automne 2008, il fit de nouveau les gros titres des journaux : avec une vente aux enchères toute entière consacrée à ses œuvres d'art, dont le clou fut « Le Veau d'Or » – un veau dans le formol partiellement revêtu d'or, vendu pour plus de 14 millions de dollars.

Een tijgerhaai in formaldehyde, een schaap op dezelfde wijze geconserveerd, of een in diamant gezette schedel – zijn kunstobjecten maken van Damian Hirst al sinds einde jaren tachtig van de vorige eeuw een veelbesproken schandaalkunstenaar. In het najaar van 2008 haalde hij opnieuw de krantenkoppen naar aanleiding van een veiling die volledig aan de verkoop van zijn kunstwerken was gewijd. Eén van de hoogtepunten van de veiling was "Het Gouden Kalf" – een jonge stier geconserveerd in formaldehyde en deels versierd met goud. Het werd voor meer dan $ 14 miljoen dollar verkocht.

the most expensive stamp ever

November 1996, David Feldman SA, Zurich, SWITZERLAND

The "Treskilling Yellow" is considered to the rarest and most expensive stamp in the world. What makes it so special is the fact that it's not supposed to be yellow at all. Back in 1855, the 3-shilling stamp from Sweden was actually green-blue. It was the 8-shilling stamp that was yellow and at, some point, a misprint must have occurred. The actual number of misprinted stamps remains unknown to this day. Only one of them has been known to circulate the market, which is why it sold for the sensational price of more than 2 million dollars at an auction in 1996.

Le « Treskilling Yellow » est reconnu comme le timbre le plus rare et le plus précieux au monde. Sa particularité est qu'il n'aurait jamais dû être jaune. En 1855, le timbre suédois de trois schillings était normalement imprimé en vert-bleu. Le jaune était réservé pour l'émission de huit schillings et il y a donc eu une erreur d'impression. On ignore aujourd'hui encore combien de timbres sont issus de cette erreur. Le marché de la philatélie n'en connaît aucun autre spécimen ; c'est pourquoi il atteignit lors de sa vente aux enchères en 1996 la somme record de 2 millions de dollars.

De "Treskilling Yellow" wordt als de zeldzaamste en duurste postzegel ter wereld beschouwd. Wat hem zo bijzonder maakt, is dat hij helemaal niet geel zou mogen zijn. In 1855 was de Zweedse zegel van 3 shilling namelijk groen-blauw, terwijl de zegel van 8 shilling geel was. Maar ergens moet er een drukfout zijn gebeurd. Tot op vandaag weet men niet hoeveel zegels er eigenlijk verkeerd gedrukt zijn. Slechts één van die zegels is op de markt; op een veiling in 1996 ging hij dan ook van de hand voor de sensationele prijs van ruim 2 miljoen dollar.

contents

rich and beautiful
01

happy birthday, mr. president // a little piece of cloth with plenty sex appeal // jimi hendrix as up close as it gets // the white album no. 0000005 // what a scary passport // holiday with mr. bean // here to save the world // elvis presley's peacock outfit // a guide to marilyn's companions // join the sgt. pepper's lonely hearts club band // dress up for a breakfast at tiffany's // no new queen for marie antoinette's pearls // the wittelsbach diamond // let's play bonnie and clyde // to be as cool as james bond // ursula, undress! // k.i.t.t. and michael part ways // fight against darth vader // worth every penny // the first lady of france—in the buff // cher's black little nothing // che guevara's revolutionary bangs

expensive
02

a true classic—the bugatti royale // double eagle—the most expensive coin // allah's words of immeasurable value // the violin of the devil's fiddler // the most expensive fossil // the magic price for words // the most expensive scrabble board // what time is it? // the most expensive baseball card // a very personal declaration of independence // the first adventure of spiderman // sex.com for millions of dollars // a very special license plate // 5 £ + auction = $ 31,200 // the most expensive bottle of wine // white truffles—edible gold // andy warhol meets velvet underground // pablo picasso's masterpiece // the world's most expensive cow // the most expensive stamp ever

curiosities
03

my holy toast // the beautiful teeth of paris hilton // there's money in cornflakes // chocolate from the south pole // britney's real gum back // a royal piece of cake // royal stockings from way back when // not tonight, josephine // what nobody needs // the luckiest phone number ever: 8x8 // what a good old beer // beam me up, scotty! // make love not war // a kid named erich honecker // adolf hitler's globe // look into the future with nostradamus // it's magic: houdini's water torture cell // buying drugs from the government // katie's top model hairstyle // a "holy" car—the pope's vw golf // one key could have saved them all // whole life for sale

locations
04

my home is my prison // the wall must go // room for a real mega party // my home, my car, my hamlet // how big: galaxy for sale // the minsk—a giant of the seven seas // be a part of disneyland—on a tombstone // a window that changed world history // stairway to heaven // anybody want to buy belgium? // big wheel keeps on turning // your name on mount mckinley // the sexiest millennium party ever

my holy toast

November 2004, eBay online

$ 28,000

What must it be like to sit down for breakfast only to realize that there's a face in your toast? Especially if it's the face of the Holy Virgin Mary? Such a "holy" toast was discovered during a simple, regular breakfast in Fort Lauderdale, Florida, in the mid 1990s. Its finder kept it as a good luck charm in a plastic bag—until selling it on eBay in November 2004 for an amazing 28,000 bucks! This auction inspired the creator of the Holy Toast Embosser, which also grants non-believers a daily spiritual calling.

Que peut-on ressentir quand on s'aperçoit au petit déjeuner que le toast que l'on mange porte l'effigie d'un visage ? Le plus étrange dans cette histoire, c'est que le visage est celui de la Vierge Marie. Ce toast « miracle » surgit au cours d'un petit déjeuner tout à fait normal au milieu des années 1990 à Fort Lauderdale en Floride. Le propriétaire conserva dans un sac en plastique cette mascotte porte-bonheur – avant de vendre le toast aux enchères en novembre 2004 sur eBay. Il s'envola pour le prix de 28 000 dollars ! Cette Vente aux enchères fut l'inspiration pour la création du « toast miracle à impression », un médium idéale pour la conversion spirituel des libres penseurs.

Hoe zou het voelen om te gaan ontbijten en vast te stellen dat er een gezicht op je toast staat? Vooral dan als het om het gezicht van de Heilige Maagd Maria gaat? Zo'n "heilige" toast werd halverwege de jaren '90 gevonden bij een simpel, gewoon ontbijt in Fort Lauderdale, Florida. De vinder hield de toast bij als geluksbrenger in een plastic zak – tot hij besloot om die in november van 2004 te verkopen op eBay voor het ongelooflijke bedrag van 28.000 dollar! Deze veiling vormde de aanzet voor de "Holy Toast Embossser", een stempel die elke snee toast voorziet van een afbeelding van de Maagd Maria en op die manier ook niet-gelovigen dagelijks op een spirituele ervaring trakteert.

the beautiful teeth of paris hilton

July 2007, BOB95fm, Fargo USA

$ 1,000

Paris Hilton—glamorous party queen and heir to the billions of the Hilton Group—is the kind of woman who knows exactly how to make her fortune even bigger. With her outrageous ideas, attractive looks and regular headlines in the tabloids, America's It-Girl has many fans who'd give anything for a personal item to remember her by. Thus, a piece of dental floss that Paris had used fetched an amazing $ 1,000 at a radio auction.

Paris Hilton, la scintillante reine de soirées jet-set et riche héritière du consortium Hilton, une multinationale qui pèse des milliards, est une femme qui sait exactement comment accroître sa fortune. Avec ses idées folles, son physique avantageux et son habitude de faire les gros titres de la presse à sensation, cette américaine en vue a de nombreux fans qui donneraient tout pour décrocher un souvenir d'elle original. C'est ainsi qu'en juillet 2007 un morceau de fil dentaire utilisé par Paris est parti pour 1 000 dollars lors d'une vente aux enchères par radio.

Paris Hilton – de glamoureuze party queen en erfgename van de miljarden van de Hilton Groep – is het soort vrouw dat precies weet hoe ze haar fortuin nog kan vergroten. Dankzij haar extravagante ideeën, fraaie snoetje en regelmatige verschijningen in de tabloids heeft de Amerikaanse It-Girl vele fans die alles over hebben voor een persoonlijk aandenken. Een stukje tandfloss van Paris ging dan ook voor een verbazingwekkende $ 1.000 van de hand bij een veiling op de radio.

© Getty Images

there's money in cornflakes

March 2008, eBay online

© Kerstin Klose

Having breakfast one day, two siblings in the U.S. found a cornflake shaped like the state of Illinois. So the two resourceful ladies took a picture of their special cornflake and began offering it on eBay. To their amazement, the prices offered for it went through the roof—until eBay interrupted the auction, because it's illegal to auction non-packaged food items. It was only through a detour in the form of auctioning a coupon for it that the siblings were able to seal the deal and finally sell their cornflake. Albeit for a lot less money—the highest bidder paid $ 1.350.

Deux sœurs américaines trouvèrent au petit déjeuner un corn-flake ayant les contours de l'état américain de l'Illinois. Les deux malignes photographièrent ce corn-flake spécial et le mirent en vente sur eBay. A leur grande surprise, le prix atteignit une somme vertigineuse – jusqu'à ce qu'eBay interrompe les enchères, car la vente aux enchères d'aliments non emballés n'est pas autorisée. Par le biais d'un bon vendu aux enchères, les deux sœurs réussirent finalement à vendre leur corn-flake. Malheureusement pour une somme bien plus modeste – le plus offrant ne paya que 1 350 dollars.

Op een dag vonden twee zussen uit de VS bij hun ontbijt een cornflake in de vorm van de staat Illinois. De twee vindingrijke dames namen dan maar een foto van hun speciale cornflake en zetten die te koop op eBay. Tot hun verbazing swingde de prijs de pan uit – tot eBay de veiling stillegde, omdat het onwettelijk is om niet-verpakte voedingsartikelen via veilingen te verkopen. Enkel via een omweg, door het veilen van een bon, konden de zussen de deal beklinken en uiteindelijk toch hun cornflake verkopen. Zij het dan voor een pak minder geld – de hoogste bieder betaalde $ 1.350.

chocolate from the south pole

September 2001, Christie's, London UK

THIS BAR OF CHOCOLATE WAS TAKEN FROM THE BOAT "DISCOVERY" ON ITS RETURN FROM CAPT: SCOTTS EXPEDITION TO ATTEMPT TO REACH THE SOUTH POLE IN 1905

$710

In the early 20th Century, Sir Ernest Henry Shackleton and Sir Robert Falcon Scott, two British polar explorers, organized expeditions into Antarctica. It doesn't take a rocket scientist to imagine that the energy of a chocolate bar is a must, particularly on an expedition such as this! That's why the two men took the sweets along with their special equipment. One of those chocolate bars remained uneaten and was stored for 100 years—only to be sold at Christie's in London for more than $ 700.

Sir Ernest Henry Shackleton et Sir Robert Falcon Scott, deux explorateurs polaires, entreprirent au début du 20ème siècle des expéditions dans l'Antarctique. On comprend aisément qu'ils aient eu besoin, pour ce type d'expédition, de l'énergie fournie par une barre chocolatée. C'est pourquoi, outre leur équipement de recherche, ils avaient emporté des friandises dans leurs bagages. Une de ces barres chocolatées ne fut pas mangée, mais conservée pendant 100 ans – et finalement vendue chez Christie's à Londres pour plus de 700 dollars.

In het begin van de 20ste eeuw organiseerden Sir Ernest Henry Shackleton en Sir Robert Falcon Scott, twee Britse poolreizigers, expedities naar Antarctica. Je hoeft geen raketwetenschapper te zijn om te weten dat de energie van een reep chocolade een must is, vooral bij dergelijke expedities! Daarom namen de twee mannen dit snoepgoed mee, naast hun speciale uitrusting. Een van die chocoladerepen werd niet opgegeten; pas 100 jaar later werd hij bij Christie's in Londen verkocht voor meer dan $ 700.

britney's real gum back

September 2004, eBay online

$ 382,81

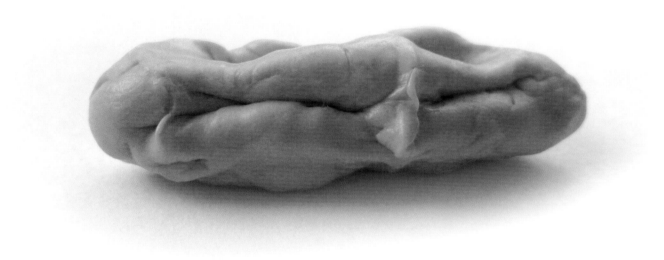

© Fotolia, Chris Gaillard

All scandals notwithstanding, she remains to many the unquestionable No. 1 of pop princesses: Britney Spears, who's stood on stages from early childhood on to become one of the most successful female stars of our time. Who would doubt then that her fans would give their last shirt for something to remember the beautiful singer by? But even her die-hard fans were flabbergasted to learn that a piece of gum chewed and spat out by Britney Spears fetched almost $ 400 on eBay.

Malgré tous les scandales qu'elle a provoqués, elle reste pour beaucoup la numéro 1 incontestée des princesses de la pop musique : Britney Spears, la blonde Américaine, montée sur scène dès son enfance et devenue ainsi l'une des stars féminines les plus célèbres au monde. Il ne fait donc aucun doute que des fans laisseraient leur chemise pour obtenir un souvenir de la belle chanteuse – mais qu'un chewing gum qu'elle a mâché et craché atteigne les 400 dollars dans une vente aux enchères étonne quand même les fans les plus mordus.

Ondanks alle schandalen blijft ze de onbetwiste nummer 1 van alle popprinsessen: Britney Spears, die al van kindsbeen af op het podium staat, is uitgegroeid tot een van de meest succesvolle vrouwelijke sterren van vandaag. Wie zou er dan ook aan twijfelen dat haar fans zich blauw zouden betalen voor een aandenken van hun favoriete zangeres? Maar zelfs de die-hard fans vielen steil achterover toen bleek dat een stukje kauwgom waarop Britney Spears had gekauwd en dat ze had uitgespuwd, voor bijna $ 400 werd verkocht op eBay.

03   **a royal piece of cake**

August 2008, Dominic Winter, Cirencester UK

Just the right auction for those fans of the British monarchy, who do not place high regard on taste! In August 2008, a piece of cake went up for auction that had been part of the wedding cake for Lady Diana and Prince Charles. An in-house employee of Queen Mum's had wrapped the piece in plastic and kept it for 27 years. After the death of Queen Mum, he decided to sell his "artifact" together with a thank-you note for the wedding present and a bottle of beer specially brewed for the occasion of Prince William's birth.

L'enchère idéale pour les fans de la famille royale britannique pour qui le bon goût a peu d'importance ! En août 2008, un morceau de gâteau provenant d'une pièce montée du mariage du Prince Charles et de Diana fut mis aux enchères. Un employé de maison de la Reine mère avait conservé, durant 27 ans, ce morceau de gâteau enveloppé dans un film plastique. Après la mort de la Reine mère, il décida de vendre ce souvenir, accompagné d'une lettre de remerciements pour le cadeau de mariage et d'une bouteille de bière brassée spécialement à l'occasion de la naissance du Prince William.

Precies de juiste veiling voor fans van de Britse monarchie die geen al te beste smaak hebben! In augustus van 2008 werd een stuk taart geveild van de bruidstaart van Lady Diana en Prins Charles. Een werknemer van de Queen Mum had de taart ingepakt in plastic en 27 jaar lang bijgehouden. Na de dood van de Queen Mum besloot hij om zijn "artefact" te verkopen, samen met een bedankbriefje voor het bruidscadeau en een flesje bier dat speciaal voor de geboorte van Prins William was gebrouwen.

$14,300

© Fotolia, Arman Zhenikeyev

royal stockings from way back when

September 2008, Hanson's Auctions, Etwall UK

© Associated Press

Hand-embroidered silk stockings retain their value even today—especially if a queen wore them. In September 2008, Hanson's Auctions offered a pair of strapless stockings owned by Queen Victoria. The queen used to wear those well-preserved silk stockings, embroidered with the royal symbol, back in the 1870s. Over 130 years later, they sold for more than 14,000 dollars. The royal stockings are now on display in a museum for textile arts in Nottingham, England.

Des bas de soie, brodés à la main, ont encore de la valeur, même de nos jours – surtout s'ils furent portés par une reine. En septembre 2008, la maison de ventes Hanson's Auctions mit en vente une paire de bas, sans jarretelle, de la Reine Victoria. La Reine avait porté ces bas, restés en très bon état et ornés avec les armoiries royales brodées, dans les années 1870. Plus de 130 ans après, les enchères pour ces bas royaux s'élevèrent à plus de 14 000 dollars. Aujourd'hui, on peut les admirer à Nottingham dans un musée consacré aux arts du tissage et du tricot.

Met de hand geborduurde zijden kousen verliezen ook vandaag hun waarde niet – en al zeker niet als ze door een koningin gedragen zijn. In september van 2008 veilde Hanson's Auctions een paar strapless kousen van Queen Victoria. De koningin droeg de goed bewaarde zijden kousen, met het koninklijke wapenschild erop geborduurd in de jaren 1870. Ruim 130 jaar later gingen ze voor meer dan 14.000 dollar van de hand. De koninklijke kousen zijn nu tentoongesteld in een museum voor de textielkunst in het Engelse Nottingham.

not tonight, josephine

1977, Christie's, London UK

© Fotolia, Bruno Delacotte

$ 38,000

In 1977 the London auction house Christie's included in its catalogue an item described as a "shrivelled object" about an inch long and looking like a shrivelled eel. The item was part of the collection of Abbot Ange Vignali, who was the priest of the late Napoleon Bonaparte on St. Helena. After Napoleon's death, the Abbot kept a few souvenirs. Among some knives and forks, Vignali took also a small piece of the fallen emperor's person. Which part exactly was never said! The highest bid, however, was made by an American urologist.

En 1977, la maison de ventes aux enchères Christie's inscrivit à son catalogue un objet d'environ 2,5 cm, intitulé « objet rétréci » et ressemblant à une anguille ratatinée. L'objet faisait partie de la collection de l'abbé Ange Vignali, le prêtre de Napoléon Bonaparte à Sainte-Hélène. À la mort de Napoléon, Vignali conserva maints souvenirs. Outre quelques couteaux et fourchettes, le curé s'appropria également un petit morceau du corps de l'empereur déchu. Nul ne dit jamais de quelle partie du corps il s'agissait. En revanche, l'enchère gagnante venait d'un urologue américain.

In 1977 stond in de catalogus van het Londense veilinghuis Christie's een item dat als een "verschrompeld voorwerp" werd omschreven, zo'n 2,5 cm lang was en er als een verschrompelde paling uitzag. Het item maakte deel uit van de collectie van abt Ange Vignali, die de priester van Napoleon Bonaparte was op St. Helena. Na de dood van Napoleon hield de abt een paar souvenirs bij. Naast enkele messen en vorken bewaarde Vignali ook een stukje van het lichaam van de gevallen keizer. Er werd nooit bij gezegd welk deel het precies was, maar het hoogste bod kwam van een Amerikaanse uroloog!

$ 1,45

Gallstones are a real pain. To the person suffering from them, they mean adhering to a rigid diet and being tormented by frequent stomach pain and, in the worst case, even by severe colic. If gallstones can't be dissolved, then they have to be surgically removed—and who wouldn't be glad to finally be rid of them? Yet, that didn't prevent someone from trying to sell his gallstones on eBay in August 2008. As it turned out, however, most people don't seem to want any—their price barely made $ 1.45.

Les calculs biliaires sont vraiment désagréables. A cause d'eux, le malade peut être obligé de suivre un régime strict ; il souffre souvent de maux de ventre et, dans le pire des cas, il est tourmenté par de graves coliques. Si les calculs ne peuvent être dissous, il faut les enlever par intervention chirurgicale – le patient est alors bien content d'en être débarrassé. En août 2008, quelqu'un mit en vente ses calculs biliaires sur eBay. Mais, comme la plupart des gens préfèrent ne pas en avoir, leur prix atteignit non sans mal 1,45 dollar.

Galstenen zijn een pijnlijke zaak. Wie er heeft, moet zich aan een strikt dieet houden en heeft vaak last van maagpijn en, in het ergste geval, ernstige kolieken. Als galstenen niet kunnen worden opgelost, moeten ze chirurgisch worden verwijderd – en wie wil er niet vanaf zijn? Toch was er iemand die in augustus van 2008 zijn galstenen probeerde te verkopen op eBay. Maar de meeste mensen moesten er niets van weten – ze gingen voor amper $ 1.45 van de hand.

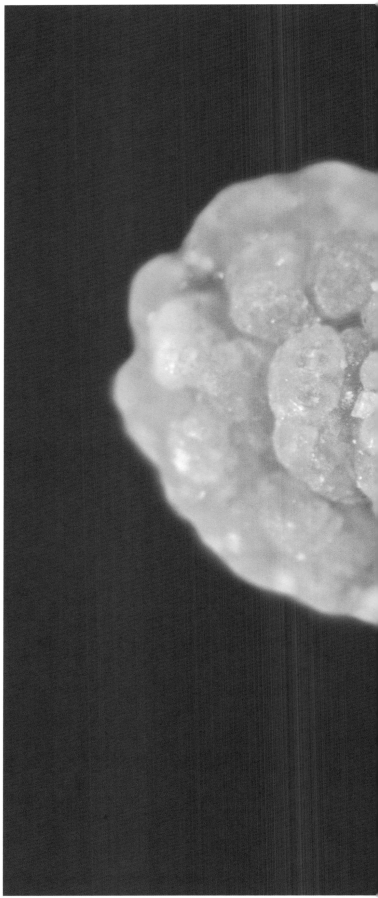

© Getty Images

the luckiest phone number ever: 8x8

August 2003, Chinese Government, Sichuan CHINA

$ 280,000

© Fotolia, Ivan Grlic

Everybody loves good luck charms—like the number eight, which many Chinese consider to be a real good luck number. So imagine the highlight in China when your phone number is 8888 8888. Rather than leave it to fate to decide who gets to consider themselves lucky every time the phone rings, the Chinese government therefore decided in August 2003 to sell this unique phone number to the highest bidder. It wasn't long before someone was willing to pay $ 280,000 for the good luck number in the hope that fortune would smile upon him.

Un porte-bonheur est une chose bien agréable – tel le chiffre 8, considéré par de nombreux Chinois comme un véritable porte-bonheur. Le summum en Chine est donc de pouvoir détenir le numéro de téléphone 8888 8888. Mais s'estimer heureux à chaque coup de téléphone n'est pas une chance que l'on peut laisser au hasard ; c'est pourquoi le gouvernement chinois a attribué au plus offrant ce numéro de téléphone unique en août 2003. Il en a coûté 280 000 dollars à l'« heureux » gagnant d'influencer positivement son destin avec ce numéro porte-bonheur.

Iedereen houdt van geluksbrengers – zoals het nummer acht, dat voor veel Chinezen een heus geluksgetal is. Je kan je dus wel voorstellen wat er in China gebeurt als je telefoonnummer 8888 8888 is. In augustus van 2003 besloot de Chinese overheid om niet het lot te laten beslissen wie zich gelukkig mocht prijzen telkens de telefoon gaat, maar om dit unieke telefoonnummer aan de hoogste bieder te verkopen. Het duurde niet lang voor iemand $ 280.000 wou neertellen voor het geluksnummer, in de hoop dat het geluk hem zou toelachen.

03 | what a good old beer

August 2007, eBay online

© Fotolia, Flavijus Philiponis

$503,300

When Sir Edward Belcher prepared the "Kane's Expedition" for Antarctica in the year 1852, he was on an important mission: He was to search and locate Sir John Franklin, who'd previously gone lost in Antarctica. To help him and his men face the cold, Allsopp Brewery created "Samuel Allsopp's Arctic Ale" —a beer that withstood arctic temperatures. One of these came up for auction at eBay in 2007—interest in the historic beverage was so enormous that its price skyrocketed to more than half a million dollars after just 157 offers.

Quand Sir Edward Belcher prépara l'expédition Kane en Arctique en 1852, il avait une mission importante : chercher et retrouver Sir John Franklin disparu depuis longtemps dans l'Arctique. Pour donner des forces à l'équipage contre le froid, la brasserie Allsopp créa la « Samuel Allsopp's Arctic Ale », une bière spéciale résistant aux températures polaires. L'une de ces bouteilles fut adjugée en 2007 sur eBay – l'intérêt pour cette boisson d'exception fut énorme et il ne fallut que 157 offres pour que le prix grimpe à plus d'un demi million de dollars.

Toen Sir Edward Belcher in het jaar 1852 bezig was met de voorbereidingen voor de "Kane Expeditie" naar Antarctica, had hij een belangrijke missie: hij moest op zoek gaan naar Sir John Franklin, die vermist was geraakt in Antarctica. Om hem en zijn mannen tegen de kou te beschermen, creëerde brouwerij Allsopp "Samuel Allsopps Poolbier" – een biertje dat tegen de pooltemperaturen bestand was. Een van die biertjes werd in 2007 op eBay geveild – de belangstelling voor het historische drankje was zo groot dat de prijs na amper 157 keer bieden meer dan een half miljoen dollar bedroeg.

beam me up, scotty

October 2008, Christie's, New York USA

$576,000

A three-day paradise shopping event delighted Star Trek fans from around the world in October 2008 at Christie's in New York. On behalf of CBS Paramount television studios, the auction house put 4,000 original requisites of the world-famous "Star Trek" movies and series up for auction. They included Mr. Spock's pointed ears as well as numerous costumes and weapons. The most expensive item sold on this occasion was an almost two-meter-long model of the famous spaceship for a cool $ 576,000.

Les fans de « Star Trek » du monde entier ont vécu trois jours de braderie mémorable en octobre 2008 chez Christie's à New York. Au nom des studios de télévision CBS Paramount, la salle de ventes a fait défiler sous le marteau 4 000 accessoires originaux provenant des films et des séries « Star Trek » célèbres sur toute la planète. Dans le lot figuraient les oreilles pointues de Mr. Spock, de nombreux costumes originaux ainsi que des armes. La pièce la plus chère cédée à cette occasion fut une maquette d'environ deux mètres de long du célèbre vaisseau spatial qui s'envola pour 576 000 dollars.

In oktober van 2008 waren Star Trek fans van over de hele wereld in de wolken naar aanleiding van een driedaags shoppingevenement bij Christie's in New York. In naam van de CBS Paramount televisiestudio's bood het veilinghuis 4.000 originele rekwisieten uit de wereldberoemde "Star Trek"-films en -series te koop aan. Het ging onder andere om de puntoren van Mr. Spock en tal van kostuums en wapens. Het duurste artikel dat werd verkocht, was een bijna twee meter lang model van het beroemde ruimteschip, dat voor een coole $ 576.000 van de hand ging.

During World War II, they were used by the Nazis before protecting the southern Bulgarian border during the Cold War—a total of 40 operational German-made tanks. Then they lost their use at some point only to sit around idle on meadows, rusting hulks overgrown with flowers and children playing on them. It wasn't until 2008 that these tanks were finally sold off—a feast for collectors of historical military equipment.

Pendant la Seconde guerre mondiale, ils furent mis en œuvre par les nazis ; ensuite, durant la guerre froide, ils protégèrent la frontière sud de la Bulgarie : 40 blindés en état de marche venant d'Allemagne. Puis, avec le temps, plus personne n'en eut l'utilisation et ils restèrent là, dans les prés, inutilisés, rouillés, envahis par les mauvaises herbes, les enfants des environs jouant dessus. En 2008, les blindés défilèrent sous le marteau du commissaire-priseur – une aubaine pour les collectionneurs d'armement militaire historique.

Tijdens Wereldoorlog II werden ze door de Nazi's gebruikt en tijdens de Koude Oorlog beschermden ze de zuidelijke grens van Bulgarije – in totaal 40 operationele Duitse tanks. Daarna werden ze overbodig en stonden ze weg te roesten in de weiden, overwoekerd door bloemen en gebruikt als speeltuigen voor kinderen. Pas in 2008 werden deze tanks uiteindelijk verkocht – een festijn voor verzamelaars van historische militaire uitrusting.

a kid named erich honecker

November 2006, eBay online

$ 5,326

© Associated Press

When he was General Secretary of the former East Germany, Erich Honecker gave his citizens plenty of reasons to respect him—as well as plenty of reasons to hate him. After he was ousted in October 1989, legal consequences for his orders to shoot refugees at the Berlin Wall forced him to flee to Moscow. A few years later, he passed away in Chile in 1994. Following his death, "Honi" became something of a controversial cult figure—which is why his original East German FDJ identification card ("Freie Deutsche Jugend" or "Free German Youth") sold for more than $ 5,000 in November 2006.

En tant que secrétaire général du parti socialiste de la RDA, Erich Honecker donna à ses concitoyens de nombreux motifs d'admiration – mais aussi beaucoup de raisons de le haïr. Après sa démission forcée en octobre 1989, il se réfugia à Moscou pour échapper aux conséquences pénales de ses ordres d'ouvrir le feu sur le mur de Berlin. Quelques années plus tard, en 1994, il mourut au Chili. Après sa mort, « Honi » devint une icône très controversée – ceci explique que sa carte de la Jeunesse libre allemande (F.D.J.) fût vendue aux enchères en novembre 2006 pour plus de 5 000 dollars.

Toen hij nog secretaris-generaal van het vroegere Oost-Duitsland was, gaf Erich Honecker zijn burgers redenen genoeg om hem te respecteren – en redenen genoeg om hem te haten. Nadat hij in oktober van 1989 was afgezet, moest hij naar Moskou vluchten omwille van de juridische gevolgen van zijn bevel om vluchtelingen neer te schieten die over de Berlijnse Muur wilden ontsnappen. Enkele jaren later overleed hij in Chili in 1994. Na zijn dood werd "Honi" een controversiële cultfiguur. Zijn originele Oost-Duitse identiteitskaart van de FDJ ("Freie Deutsche Jugend", de jeugdorganisatie van de Communistische Partij) werd in november van 2006 dan ook voor meer dan $ 5.000 verkocht.

$100,000

John Barsamian used to be a 28-year-old soldier stationed in Berchtesgaden, Germany, at the end of World War II. While clearing Hitler's power center at Obersalzberg, the young man received permission to take the "Fuehrer's" globe back home. Back home in California, he kept it in his basement—until his 91st birthday when he decided to put the globe up for auction. The historical artifact fetched a price of $ 100,000, which Barsamian used to pay off his bills and to donate to charity.

À la fin de la Seconde guerre mondiale, John Barsamian, soldat de 28 ans, était basé à Berchtesgaden. Lors de l'évacuation du quartier général de Hitler sur l'Obersalzberg, le jeune homme reçut l'autorisation d'emporter avec lui le globe terrestre du Führer. Rentré en Californie, il garda ce globe dans sa cave – jusqu'à ses 91 ans où le vétéran décida de vendre ce globe aux enchères. Ce trophée historique a trouvé preneur pour 100 000 dollars avec lesquels Barsamian paya quelques factures et fit un don à une œuvre de charité.

Aan het eind van Wereldoorlog II was John Barsamian als 28-jarige soldaat in het Duitse Berchtesgaden gelegerd. Bij het opruimen van Hitlers machtscentrum op de Obersalzberg kreeg de jongeman de toestemming om de wereldbol van de Führer mee naar huis te nemen. Eens hij weer thuis was in California, borg hij de wereldbol in zijn kelder op – tot aan zijn 91ste verjaardag. Toen besloot hij om de bol te laten veilen. Het historische artefact ging van de hand voor $ 100.000, een bedrag dat Barsamian gebruikte om zijn schulden te betalen. De rest ging naar liefdadigheid.

look into the future with nostradamus

April 2007, Swann Auction Galleries, New York USA

$13,200

16th-Century French astrologist Nostradamus published numerous writings that are regarded as a glimpse into the future. They remain a mystery to this day as a whole range of scientists is still trying to uncover his messages. Hence, there was great interest when a library devoted to Nostradamus went up for auction in New York in April 2007. The greatest attention went to the first and only still existing prognosis of the future, written by Nostradamus himself in 1568—it sold for the sensational price of $13,200.

L'astrologue français Nostradamus qui vécut au 16ème siècle rédigea de nombreux écrits considérés comme des prophéties. Aujourd'hui encore, celles-ci restent mystérieuses et une multitude de scientifiques se consacrent encore au déchiffrage de ses prévisions. La mise en vente aux enchères d'une bibliothèque consacré à Nostradamus en avril 2007 à New York suscita donc un vif intérêt. La première prophétie de Nostradamus de l'année 1568 était assurément la plus intéressante – elle atteignit l'enchère record de 13 200 dollars.

De 16de-eeuwse, Franse astroloog Nostradamus publiceerde tal van werken die als een blik op de toekomst worden beschouwd. Het mysterie is nog altijd niet ontsluierd; ook vandaag nog proberen tal van wetenschappers zijn boodschappen te ontrafelen. De belangstelling was dan ook groot toen een bibliotheek gewijd aan Nostradamus in april 2007 onder de hamer ging in New York. De meeste aandacht ging naar de eerste en enige overlevende toekomstvoorspelling, van de hand van Nostradamus zelf uit 1568 – die ging voor de sensationele prijs van $13.200 van de hand.

PROGNOSTICATION

nouuelle, & prediction por-
tenteuſe, pour Lan
M. D. LV.

Compoſee par maiſtre Michel Noſtradamus,
docteur en medicine, de Salon de Craux en Pro-
uence, nommee par Ammianus Marcelinus
SALVVIVM.

Dicata Heroico præſuli D. IOSEPHO *des Paniſſes,
Caualiſſenſi præpoſito.*

M. DE
NOSTRE
DAME.

A Lyon, par Iean Brotot.

it's magic: houdini's water torture cell

October 2004, Liberace Museum, Las Vegas USA

$ 300,000

At the turn of the century, Harry Houdini was one of the greatest magicians and escape artists of his time. One way he used to fascinate his audience was with sophisticated escape acts—including the one in which he freed himself from a straight jacket while being suspended in it from a skyscraper. One spectacle repeated to this day was his escape from chains under water. In October 2004, his "Water Torture Cell" constructed for just that purpose was sold to the highest bidder for $ 300,000 in Las Vegas.

Au tournant du 20ème siècle, Harry Houdini était l'un des plus grands prestidigitateurs et briseurs de chaînes de son temps. Le public était fasciné par ses tours à la mise en scène dramatique où il se débarrassait de ses chaînes – il parvint ainsi à s'extraire d'une camisole de force, suspendu à un filin du haut d'un gratte-ciel. Le numéro consistant à se libérer de ses liens sous l'eau est un spectacle que l'on continue d'imiter aujourd'hui encore. La « Chambre aux Tortures immergée » spécialement construite à cet effet fut vendue en octobre 2004 à Las Vegas au meilleur enchérisseur pour 300 000 dollars.

Rond de eeuwwisseling was Harry Houdini één van de grootste illusionisten en ontsnappingskunstenaars van zijn tijd. Een van de manieren waarop hij zijn publiek boeide, waren gesofistikeerde ontsnappingstrucs – zoals een truc waarbij hij zichzelf uit een dwangbuis bevrijdde terwijl hij ondersteboven aan een wolkenkrabber hing. Een andere proef die ook vandaag nog wordt gedaan, is een onderwaterontsnapping terwijl men vastgeketend is. In oktober van 2004 werd zijn "watertank", die precies daarvoor gebouwd was, in Las Vegas aan de hoogste bieder voor $ 300.000 verkocht.

buying drugs from the government

August 2003, US Government, San Diego USA

TOO MUCH

The US Government auctions off impounded vehicles on a regular basis—which can include real bargains for buyers. Two Tijuana-based printers used such an opportunity and purchased a vehicle they intended to bring back to Mexico. At the border, however, customs officials discovered 19 pounds of marihuana in the car and promptly put the two men in jail. Luckily it turned out that the dope had been missed during the original search of the car and the two printers were set free. Still, they never intend to buy a car from that source again.

Le gouvernement américain vend régulièrement aux enchères des véhicules confisqués – c'est l'occasion de faire de bonnes affaires. Deux imprimeurs originaires de Tijuana en profitèrent pour acquérir une voiture qu'ils comptaient ramener dans leur pays, le Mexique. Mais à la frontière, les douaniers y découvrirent 19 livres de marijuana et mirent tout de suite les deux hommes en prison. Heureusement, on se rendit vite compte que la marijuana avait échappé à la vigilance des autorités de l'état lors de l'enquête et les deux ouvriers furent libérés. Ils ne se risqueront sûrement plus jamais à acheter une voiture aux enchères.

De Amerikaanse overheid veilt regelmatig in beslag genomen voertuigen en soms zitten daar echte koopjes tussen. Twee drukkers uit Tijuana maakten van die gelegenheid gebruik om een auto te kopen die ze terug naar Mexico wilden brengen. Maar aan de grens vond de douane 9 kilo marihuana in de auto. De twee mannen werden onmiddellijk in de gevangenis gestopt. Gelukkig voor hen bleek dat de drugs over het hoofd waren gezien bij de oorspronkelijke doorzoeking van de auto. De twee drukkers werden dan ook vrijgelaten. Toch gaan ze nooit meer een auto van de Amerikaanse overheid kopen.

katie's top model hairstyle

July 2008, eBay online

$ 1,025

Even top models run into bad luck sometimes. Like Kate Moss at the Hotel Adlon in Berlin in the summer of 2008 when she attempted to dodge some paparazzi—at the expense of some artificial strands of hair. One of the paparazzi immediately snatched the strands and put them up for sale on eBay. That's where German TV show host Niels Ruf laid down a solid $ 1,000 in order to boost his ratings with the strands, while the resourceful boulevard photographer donated his share to an anti-drug organization.

Même les mannequins vedettes ont quelquefois la poisse. Comme Kate Moss en cet été 2008 où elle dut fuir pour échapper aux paparazzis à l'hôtel Adlon de Berlin – elle y laissa une mèche de faux cheveux. L'un des photographes s'empara immédiatement de ce trophée et le mit tout de suite aux enchères sur eBay. L'animateur allemand Niels Ruf, qui souhaitait donner du punch à son émission, le remporta pour un peu plus de 1 000 dollars. Tandis que l'ingénieux paparazzi reversait la recette à une organisation de lutte contre la drogue.

Zelfs topmodellen hebben al eens pech. Zoals Kate Moss die in de zomer van 2008 enkele paparazzi probeerde te ontlopen in het Berlijnse Adlon hotel – ten koste van enkele strengen kunsthaar. Een van de paparazzi raapte onmiddellijk de strengen op en zette ze te koop op eBay. Om zijn kijkcijfers op te krikken met dat haar, legde tv-presentator Niels Ruf een goede $ 1.000 op tafel, terwijl de slimme boulevardfotograaf zijn deel aan een organisatie voor drugspreventie schonk.

© Getty Images

a "holy" car—the pope's vw golf

March 2005, eBay online

$ 250,000

© Getty Images

Picture a young man going to a used-car dealer to purchase a Volkswagen Golf. From its title, he learns that the car used to belong to a clergyman. He doesn't think much of it until a couple of days later when the previous owner suddenly becomes a household name: The clergyman in question has just been named Benedict XVI to become head of the Catholic Church. Believe it or not, the story's true—and a financial blessing for the young man! In the end, he was able to sell the bargain-priced car for almost $ 250,000.

Un jeune homme se rend chez un vendeur de voitures d'occasion pour acheter une Golf. Sur les papiers, il voit que la voiture avait auparavant été conduite par un ecclésiastique. Il n'y pense plus – jusqu'à ce que, peu après, l'ancien propriétaire soit dans toutes les bouches : l'ecclésiastique n'était autre que le pape Benoît XVI fraîchement élu chef de l'église catholique. Voilà une histoire à peine croyable et pourtant véridique – et financièrement une véritable bénédiction ! Le jeune homme réussit à vendre aux enchères cette voiture acquise à un prix avantageux pour presque 250 000 dollars.

Beeldt u zich eens in: een jongeman gaat een Volkswagen Golf kopen bij een dealer in occasiewagens. Uit het eigendomsbewijs maakt hij op dat de auto van een geestelijke was. Hij staat er verder niet bij stil, tot de vorige eigenaar enkele dagen later een bekende naam wordt: als Benedictus XVI komt de geestelijke in kwestie namelijk aan het hoofd van de Katholieke Kerk te staan. Of u het nu gelooft of niet, het verhaal is waar – en ook een financiële meevaller voor de jongeman! Uiteindelijk kon hij zijn koopje voor bijna $ 250.000 van de hand doen.

one key could have saved them all

September 2007, Henry Aldridge & Son, Devizes UK

$ 210,000

When the Titanic went on her fatal maiden voyage on April 10th, 1912, somebody made a minor mistake of potentially dramatic consequences. The key to the box containing the binoculars was left in the pocket of an officer's jacket who'd been ordered off ship prior to the voyage. This left the crewmembers on the Titanic's observation mast to scan the nocturnal environment relying on plain eyesight alone. That key was kept by the officer as a memento before passing it on to his daughter. In September 2007, it ultimately sold for $ 210,000 at an auction.

Quand le Titanic leva l'ancre le 10 avril 1912 pour un voyage inaugural qui s'avéra mortel, se produisit une petite erreur aux conséquences peut-être dramatiques : la clé de l'armoire recelant les jumelles se trouvait dans la poche de veste de l'officier qui reçut une autre affectation juste avant le voyage. Des postes d'observation du Titanic, l'équipage du navire ne pouvait donc scruter les environs dans l'obscurité qu'à l'œil nu. Cette clé fut conservée par l'officier comme souvenir, remise à sa fille et finalement vendue aux enchères en septembre 2007 pour plus de 210 000 dollars.

Toen de Titanic op 10 april 1912 afvoer voor haar fatale eerste reis, maakte iemand een kleine fout die dramatische gevolgen zou hebben. De sleutel van de kist waarin de verrekijker werd bewaard, bleef in de vestzak van een officier zitten die vóór het vertrek het schip moest verlaten. Daarom konden de bemanningsleden in de observatiemast van de Titanic enkel met hun eigen ogen de nachtelijke horizon afzoeken. De officier hield de sleutel bij als aandenken en gaf hem later aan zijn dochter. In september van 2007 werd hij uiteindelijk geveild voor $ 210.000.

© Fotolia, Peter Högström

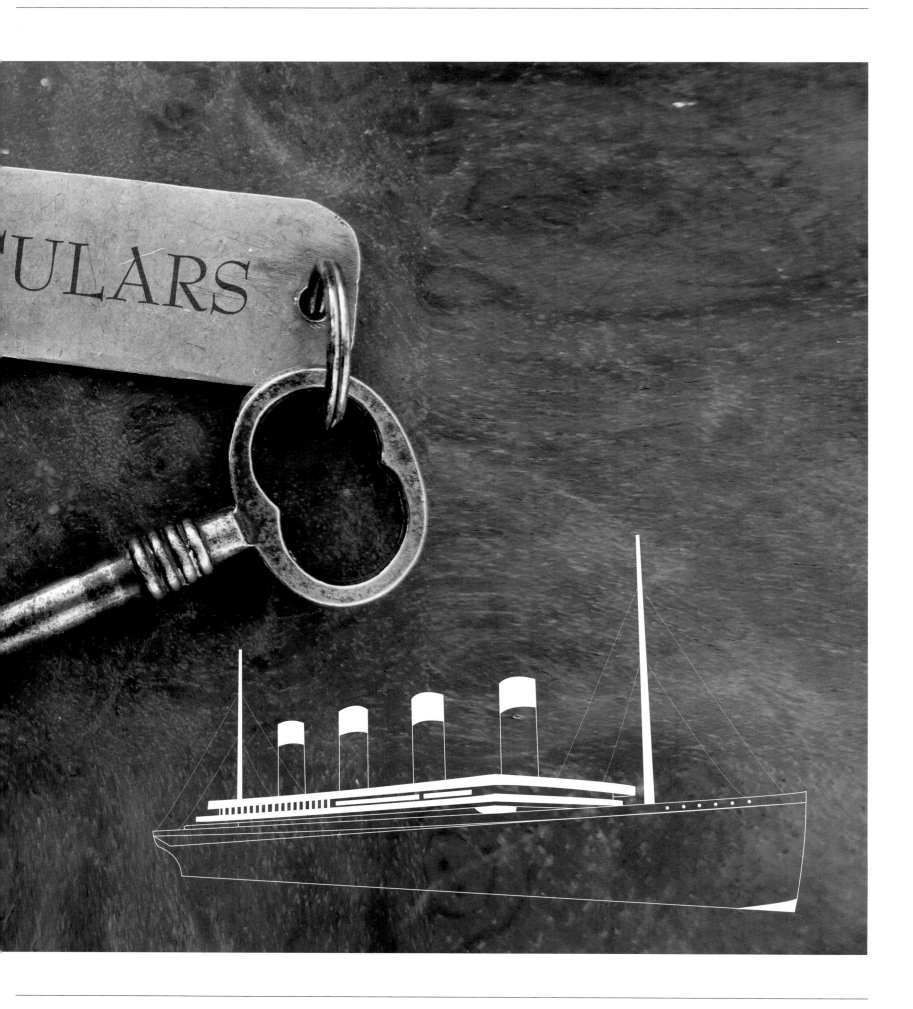

03 | whole life for sale

June 2008, eBay online

© Fotolia, Andy Dean

$ 399,300

Mr. Usher, a native of England, was living an exciting life—all kinds of interesting jobs, his own businesses, and lots of traveling. One day, after he'd found the woman of his dreams, he emigrated with her to Australia on the notion that he'd spend the rest of his days there in happiness. That is, until she left him from one day to the next. That was when he lost all interest in living in the home they used to share and he decided to sell his whole life on eBay—his job, house and friends included. The selling price reached almost $ 400,000. Talk about nice capital for a fresh start!

Usher, citoyen britannique d'origine, menait une vie palpitante – des emplois intéressants en pagaille, des affaires, de nombreux voyages. Quand il eut enfin trouvé la femme de ses rêves, il émigra avec elle en Australie où il pensait couler des jours heureux. Jusqu'au jour où celle-ci le quitta du jour au lendemain. À partir de là, il eut assez de cette vie dans ce qui avait été leur maison commune et décida donc de mettre sa vie aux enchères sur eBay – comme un tout incluant emploi, maison et amis. Le prix de vente se chiffra à presque 400 000 dollars. Un joli pécule pour commencer une nouvelle vie !

De Engelsman Usher had een opwindend leven – verschillende interessante jobs, zijn eigen ondernemingen en veel reizen. Maar op een dag vond hij de vrouw van zijn dromen en emigreerde hij met haar naar Australië, in de veronderstelling dat hij de rest van zijn dagen gelukkig met haar zou doorbrengen. Helaas, ze verliet hem van de ene dag op de andere. Daarop verloor hij al zijn belangstelling voor hun huis en besloot hij om zijn hele leven te verkopen op eBay – zijn baan, huis en vrienden inbegrepen. De uiteindelijke verkoopprijs bedroeg bijna $ 400.000. Als dat geen leuk beginkapitaal voor een nieuwe start is!

contents

rich and beautiful   01

happy birthday, mr. president // a little piece of cloth with plenty sex appeal // jimi hendrix as up close as it gets // the white album no. 0000005 // what a scary passport // holiday with mr. bean // here to save the world // elvis presley's peacock outfit // a guide to marilyn's companions // join the sgt. pepper's lonely hearts club band // dress up for a breakfast at tiffany's // no new queen for marie antoinette's pearls // the wittelsbach diamond // let's play bonnie and clyde // to be as cool as james bond // ursula, undress! // k.i.t.t. and michael part ways // fight against darth vader // worth every penny // the first lady of france—in the buff // cher's black little nothing // che guevara's revolutionary bangs

expensive   02

a true classic—the bugatti royale // double eagle—the most expensive coin // allah's words of immeasurable value // the violin of the devil's fiddler // the most expensive fossil // the magic price for words // the most expensive scrabble board // what time is it? // the most expensive baseball card // a very personal declaration of independence // the first adventure of spiderman // sex.com for millions of dollars // a very special license plate // 5 £ + auction = $ 31,200 // the most expensive bottle of wine // white truffles—edible gold // andy warhol meets velvet underground // pablo picasso's masterpiece // the world's most expensive cow // the most expensive stamp ever

curiosities   03

my holy toast // the beautiful teeth of paris hilton // there's money in cornflakes // chocolate from the south pole // britney's real gum back // a royal piece of cake // royal stockings from way back when // not tonight, josephine // what nobody needs // the luckiest phone number ever: 8x8 // what a good old beer // beam me up, scotty! // make love not war // a kid named erich honecker // adolf hitler's globe // look into the future with nostradamus // it's magic: houdini's water torture cell // buying drugs from the government // katie's top model hairstyle // a "holy" car—the pope's vw golf // one key could have saved them all // whole life for sale

locations   04

my home is my prison // the wall must go // room for a real mega party // my home, my car, my hamlet // how big: galaxy for sale // the minsk—a giant of the seven seas // be a part of disneyland—on a tombstone // a window that changed world history // stairway to heaven // anybody want to buy belgium? // big wheel keeps on turning // your name on mount mckinley // the sexiest millennium party ever

my home is my prison

December 2007, Karhausen Auctions, Berlin GERMANY

$397,000

The Republic of East Germany is now part of history. However, the dark side of its era includes, among others, its history of jailing numerous people for their political affiliations. One building that bears witness to that history is East Germany's second largest prison for political prisoners in the city of Cottbus. Following the demise of the Republic of East Germany, the prison remained unused for decades until it was put up for auction in 2007. An investor purchased this unusual piece of real estate for almost $ 400,000.

La RDA est entrée dans l'histoire. Les zones d'ombre de cette période sont habitées entre autres par les nombreux prisonniers qui furent incarcérés en raison de leur orientation politique. Le bâtiment qui en témoigne est la deuxième plus importante prison pour détenus politiques de l'ex-RDA à Cottbus. Après la fin de la RDA, cet établissement pénitentiaire resta inoccupé pendant de nombreuses années et fut vendu aux enchères en 2007. Un investisseur fit l'acquisition de ce bien immobilier inhabituel pour quelque 400 000 dollars.

De Oost-Duitse Republiek behoort nu tot het verleden. Een van de donkere zijden van dat tijdperk was de opsluiting van tal van mensen vanwege hun politieke overtuiging. De op één na grootste gevangenis van Oost-Duitsland voor politieke gevangenen in de stad Cottbus is een stille getuige van die geschiedenis. Na de teloorgang van de Oost-Duitse Republiek stond de gevangenis decennialang leeg, tot ze in 2007 werd geveild. Een investeerder kocht het ongewone stukje vastgoed voor bijna $ 400.000.

04 the wall must go

September 2008, Deutsche Grundstücksauktionen, Berlin GERMANY

$10,120

© Fotolia, Masterric 3000

The Berlin Wall wasn't exactly the best part of the city's history, considering how it separated East and West Berlin for 28 long years. Add to that that numerous people were killed in their attempts to climb over it. These facts by themselves, however, give the Wall its great historical significance, and only a few pieces of it have survived well preserved. One large piece, covered with graffiti, went up for auction in September 2008. One company bought it for at least $ 10,000, intending to put it on display in its office space.

On ne peut pas dire que le mur de Berlin soit un morceau glorieux de l'histoire de la ville car il sépara pendant plus de 28 ans la partie est et la partie ouest de Berlin. De plus, nombre de ceux qui essayèrent de passer par-dessus furent tués. C'est pour cette raison que c'est un souvenir historique important dont il ne reste plus que quelques morceaux bien conservés. En septembre 2008, un gros morceau décoré de graffitis fut mis en vente aux enchères. C'est une entreprise qui se l'adjugea pour 10 000 dollars. Le morceau de mur doit y être exposé comme un objet d'art dans les bureaux.

De Berlijnse Muur was niet echt het beste uit de geschiedenis van de stad: 28 jaar lang verdeelde hij Oost- en West-Berlijn. Bovendien werden tal van mensen gedood toen ze probeerden erover te klimmen. Het zijn deze feiten die de Muur zo historisch belangrijk maken. Toch bleven maar een paar stukken goed bewaard. In september van 2008 werd een groot stuk geveild, beschilderd met graffiti. Een onderneming kocht het voor minstens $ 10.000, met de bedoeling om het in haar kantoren tentoon te stellen.

© Martin Nicholas Kunz

$17,430

What makes a great party—100 guests? 500 guests? Why not take it all the way? 76,000 guests at the Olympiastadion in Berlin! As part of a charity event in August 2004, the German express mail company DHL sold the highest bidder the right to use Berlin's Olympic Stadium any way he or she chose for one day. Say, for an absolute mega party or even a romantic candlelight dinner just for two in the whole wide stadium—whichever mood struck the buyer who ended up spending almost 20 grand for that day.

Qu'est-ce qu'une grande soirée – une soirée avec 100 ou 500 invités ? Ou une soirée qui remplit carrément le stade olympique de Berlin avec 76 000 invités ? Dans le cadre d'une œuvre de bienfaisance, l'entreprise de transport express DHL mit aux enchères en août 2004 le droit pour le meilleur enchérisseur d'utiliser à sa guise, pendant une journée, le stade olympique berlinois. Pour organiser par exemple une gigantesque surprise-partie ou bien un romantique dîner aux chandelles pour deux amoureux, planté au milieu de l'immense stade – au choix de l'acheteur qui remporta l'enchère pour presque 20 000 dollars.

Wanneer mag je van een groot feest spreken? Bij 100 gasten? 500 gasten? Waarom zou je niet nog veel verder gaan? 76.000 gasten in het Olympiastadion in Berlijn bijvoorbeeld! In het kader van een liefdadigheidsevenement in augustus 2004 verkocht de Duitse spoedbesteller DHL aan de hoogste bieder het recht om het Olympiastadion op gelijk welke manier te gebruiken voor één dag. Voor een absolute megaparty bijvoorbeeld, of voor een romantisch etentje bij kaarslicht voor twee in het hele stadion – naar goeddunken van de koper die voor die dag bijna 20.000 dollar over had.

my home, my car, my hamlet

November 2007, eBay online

$3,300,000

© Fotolia, Alexander Reitter

A post office, a dance hall, a barn, one single home and about 60,000 square meters of land—that's the little, very little town of Albert, Texas. Founded 130 years ago, it was a virtual ghost town when the previous owner purchased it and turned it into a neat and charming weekend destination. In November 2007, however, he decided he had enough of the country life in his little town, putting its buildings and city limits up for sale on eBay. An Italian bidder secured ownership of the quaint little town for more then $ 3 million.

Un bureau de poste, une salle de danse, un hangar, une unique maison d'habitation et quelque 60 000 mètres carrés de terrain – c'est le petit, très petit village d'Albert au Texas. Cette bourgade, vieille de 130 ans, avait déjà été désertée par ses habitants quand l'ancien propriétaire l'acheta et la transforma en un charmant lieu de villégiature bien entretenu pour ex-cursionnistes en week-end. En novembre 2007, il eut assez de cette vie de cow-boy dans son petit village et mit les bâtiments, terrain compris, aux enchères sur eBay. Un enchérisseur italien gagna cet endroit idylli-que pour plus de 3 millions de dollars.

Een postkantoor, een balzaal, een schuur, één enkel huis en zo'n 60.000 vierkante meter land – dat is het piepkleine dorpje Albert in Texas. Het werd 130 jaar geleden gesticht en was nagenoeg een spookstad toen de vorige eigenaar het kocht en tot een gezel-lige en charmante weekendbestemming omtoverde. Maar in november van 2007 besloot hij dat hij genoeg had van het plattelandsleven in zijn dorpje en zette de gebouwen en het grondgebied te koop op eBay. Een Italiaanse koper verwierf het pittoreske dorpje voor ruim $ 3 miljoen.

© Fotolia, Mark Apelt

© Fotolia, Sandor Jackal

© Fotolia, Howard

In February 2008, a Canadian offered to sell a galaxy 11.6 million light years away from Earth on eBay. The galaxy comprised several thousands of stars and a black hole with 75 million times the mass of our Sun. The new owner was entitled to call himself "the rightful governor and overlord of Galaxy M81". It was pointed out, however, that any possible inhabitants of M81 had yet to approve their new "governor". It wasn't long before eBay terminated the Canadian's futuristic auction.

En février 2008, un Canadien mit en vente sur eBay une galaxie située à 11,6 millions d'années lumière. La galaxie était composée de plusieurs milliers d'étoiles et d'un trou noir super-massif de plus de 75 millions de masses solaires. Le nouveau propriétaire aurait pu porter le titre de « Gouverneur de droit et Maître de la Galaxie M81 ». On objecta que les éventuels habitants de la M81 n'avaient pas encore donné leur accord pour un nouveau gouverneur. eBay mit rapidement un terme à cette enchère futuriste.

In februari 2008 bood een Canadees een melkweg-stelsel op 11,6 miljoen lichtjaren van de aarde te koop aan op eBay. Dat melkwegstelsel telde enkele dui-zenden sterren en een zwart gat dat 75 miljoen keer de massa van onze zon heeft. De nieuwe eigenaar mocht zich "de rechtmatige gouverneur en heerser van Melkwegstelsel M81" noemen. Wel werd erop gewezen dat de mogelijke bewoners van M81 hun nieuwe "gouverneur" nog moesten goedkeuren. Het duurde niet lang voor eBay de futuristische veiling van de Canadees stillegde.

04

the minsk—a giant of the seven seas

May 2006, Xutongda Auctions, Guangdong CHINA

$ 16,000,000

It measures 273.1 meters in length, 31 meters in width, it has a top speed of 32 knots, it comes equipped with numerous twin blasters, rocket launchers, torpedo launchers and with 20 VTOL planes as well as 21 helicopters. So much for the basic data of the Russian aircraft carrier "Minsk". In service from 1978 to 1994, the vessel was originally supposed to be scrapped. Although all its weapons, communication devices as well as its engine were indeed destroyed, the ship itself was then to be put up for auction. After the auction fell through, it ended up being sold to China for $ 16 million.

273,1 mètres de long, 31 mètres de large, filant jusqu'à 32 nœuds, armé de plusieurs doubles rampes lance-missiles, de lance-roquettes et de tubes lance-torpilles, embarquant 20 chasseurs à décollage vertical et 21 hélicoptères : telles sont les caractéristiques du porte-avions russe « Minsk ». Le navire, qui fut en service de 1978 à 1994, était ensuite destiné à la ferraille. Toutes les armes, les appareils de communication ainsi que l'unité de propulsion furent effectivement détruits, mais le navire même devait être vendu aux enchères. Après l'échec de cette vente, il fut finalement cédé à la Chine pour 16 millions de dollars.

Hij is 273,1 meter lang, 31 meter breed, heeft een topsnelheid van 32 knopen en is uitgerust met tal van raketlanceerders, torpedobuizen en 20 VTOL-vliegtuigen plus 21 helikopters. Tot zover de basisgegevens van het Russische vliegdekschip "Minsk". Het vaartuig, dat van 1978 tot 1994 in dienst was, zou aanvankelijk op de schroothoop belanden. Hoewel alle wapens, communicatie-apparatuur en motoren er al uit waren gehaald, werd het schip toch nog geveild. Toen de veiling mislukte, werd het schip aan China verkocht voor $ 16 miljoen.

be a part of disneyland—on a tombstone

October 2004, eBay online

© Fotolia, Npolo Guy

$37,400

Disneyland in Anaheim, California, is among the most frequently visited adventure parks in the world. Established in the 1950s, the park is thus a popular attraction—and what could be nicer than having your own name immortalized there. On that account, a charity auction offered to the public to have one's own personally dedicated tombstone at the "Haunted Mansion" of the fun park. A physician from Louisiana decided to seize the opportunity, securing that tombstone for himself for almost $ 40,000.

Disneyland à Anaheim en Californie est l'un des parcs d'attractions les plus visités au monde. Le parc, qui fut installé dès les années 50, est donc une excursion très attrayante – quoi de plus alléchant dans ces conditions que d'y être immortalisé. À l'occasion d'une vente de charité, on proposa donc au gagnant sa propre pierre tombale avec épitaphe personnelle dans la « Maison hantée » du parc d'attractions. Un médecin originaire de Louisiane sauta sur l'occasion et obtint sa pierre pour presque 40 000 dollars.

Disneyland in Anaheim, California, is een van de drukst bezochte pretparken ter wereld. Het park, dat in de jaren '50 zijn deuren opende, is dan ook een populaire trekpleister. En wat zou er leuker kunnen zijn dan je eigen naam daar vereeuwigd te zien staan? Daarom kreeg het grote publiek tijdens een veiling de kans om zijn eigen grafsteen te bezitten bij het "spookhuis" van het pretpark. Een dokter uit Louisiana besloot zijn kans te grijpen en sleepte die grafsteen in de wacht voor bijna $ 40.000.

$3,000,000

November 22nd, 1963, changed not only America but also the whole world. That was the day when President John F. Kennedy was assassinated in Dallas, Texas. His killer, Lee Harvey Oswald, fired the deadly shots from a building on Elm Street just as the motorcade carrying the president and several other government officials passed by. For years afterward, the window from which the shots were fired remained on display in a museum. In February 2007, it was sold off at an eBay auction—for the exorbitant price of over 3 million dollars.

Le 22 novembre 1963 transforma l'Amérique mais aussi le monde entier. C'est ce jour-là que fut perpétré à Dallas, au Texas, l'attentat contre le président John F. Kennedy. Le meurtrier supposé, Lee Harvey Oswald, tira les coups mortels d'une maison située dans la rue Elm Street où défilaient les voitures du président et des autres membres du gouvernement. La fenêtre d'où l'attentat fut commis fut longtemps exposée dans un musée. En février 2007, elle fut vendue aux enchères sur eBay où elle atteignit le prix faramineux de plus de 3 millions de dollars.

Op 22 november 1963 veranderde niet alleen Amerika, maar ook de hele wereld. Op die dag werd namelijk President John F. Kennedy vermoord in het Texaanse Dallas. Zijn moordenaar Lee Harvey Oswald vuurde de dodelijke schoten af vanuit een gebouw in Elm Street, net op het moment dat de autocolonne met de president en verschillende overheidsambtenaren langsreed. Het raam van waaruit de schoten werden afgevuurd, was jaren lang te zien in een museum. In februari van 2007 werd het geveild op eBay – voor het exorbitante bedrag van ruim 3 miljoen dollar.

© Martin Nicholas Kunz

$717,350

Whenever we think of Paris, we immediately picture wide boulevards, 19th-Century architecture, cafés—and, of course, the Eiffel Tower. The landmark of Paris was built from 1887 to 1889 by Alexandre Gustave Eiffel with 1,710 stairs, which brought visitors to the top platform of the 324.82-meter tower. In 1983, the original stairway was replaced, broken down into 24 parts and sold to museums as well as collectors. When one of these parts went up for auction at Sotheby's in 2008, it changed ownership for north of $ 700,000.

Quand on pense à Paris, on voit tout de suite les grands boulevards, les immeubles Haussmann, les cafés – et naturellement la tour Eiffel. Cet emblème de Paris, construit entre 1887 et 1889 par Alexandre Gustave Eiffel, comporte 1710 marches permettant aux visiteurs d'accéder à la plate-forme supérieure, située sous l'antenne qui s'élève à 324,82 m de haut. En 1983, l'escalier d'origine dut être remplacé. Il fut divisé en 24 morceaux et vendu à des musées et des collectionneurs. Quand un de ces morceaux d'escalier fut vendu aux enchères chez Sotheby's en 2008, il changea de main pour plus de 700 000 dollars.

Wie aan Parijs denkt, ziet onmiddellijk brede boulevards, 19de-eeuwse architectuur en cafés voor zich – en natuurlijk de Eiffeltoren. Deze Parijse bezienswaardigheid werd tussen 1887 en 1889 gebouwd door Alexandre Gustave Eiffel; de 1.710 trappen brengen bezoekers naar het hoogste platform van de 324,82 meter hoge toren. In 1983 werd de originele trap vervangen, opgesplitst in 24 delen en verkocht aan musea en verzamelaars. Toen een van die delen in 2008 onder de hamer ging bij Sotheby's, veranderde het voor meer dan $ 700.000 van eigenaar.

© Michelle Galindo

does anybody wants to buy belgium?

September 2007, eBay online

After Belgium had spent one hundred days of parliamentary elections and still come up short of a government formation, a former journalist offered his home country for sale on eBay. He based his sales pitch on all kinds of interesting pros and cons about his country, including its national debt of 300 billion Euros. Nevertheless, it only took 26 offers to raise the selling price from one to more than $ 12 million—before eBay put an end to this politically dubious auction.

Après qu'aucun gouvernement n'eut pu être formé en Belgique, même cent jours après les élections parlementaires, un ancien journaliste mit son pays en vente sur eBay. Le texte de présentation était truffé d'informations intéressantes sur les qualités et les défauts du pays, tels que la dette de l'état de 300 milliards de dollars. Le prix de vente grimpa malgré tout, en seulement 26 enchères, de un à plus de 12 millions de dollars – jusqu'à ce qu'eBay mette un terme à cette enchère politiquement douteuse.

Toen België, 100 dagen na de parlementaire verkiezingen, nog altijd geen regering had, besloot een ex-journalist zijn thuisland te koop aan te bieden op eBay. In zijn verkooppraatje had hij het over alle voor- en nadelen van zijn land, waaronder de nationale schuld van 300 miljard euro. Toch steeg de verkoopprijs na amper 26 keer bieden van één naar ruim $ 12 miljoen – tot eBay een eind maakte aan deze politiek dubieuze veiling.

stopped at
$ 12,838,503

FOR SALE

© Kerstin Klose

big wheel keeps on turning

April 2008, eBay online

It has gone through more than three million rides and has become a minor celebrity—the original Ferris Wheel of Santa Monica Pier in California. It was built in 1996 and converted in 1998 to become the first Ferris wheel powered by solar energy. Its 20 gondolas offered several million people a view of the Pacific—until a new Ferris wheel was set to replace it in the year 2008. Therefore the old but well preserved Ferris wheel was sold on eBay at a steal of only $ 130,000.

Elle a fait plus de trois millions de tours et c'est une petite célébrité : la grande roue sur le quai de Santa Monica en Californie. Construite en 1996, elle devint en 1998 la première grande roue à entraînement solaire. Dans ses 20 gondoles, plusieurs millions de visiteurs purent admirer le panorama sur l'océan Pacifique – jusqu'à ce qu'en 2008 une grande roue plus moderne vînt remplacer l'ancienne. C'est pourquoi la vieille grande roue, toujours en très bon état, fut vendue aux enchères sur eBay et trouva preneur au prix dérisoire de seulement 130 000 dollars.

Het heeft er al meer dan drie miljoen ritjes op zitten en is een beroemdheid op zich – het originele Ferris Wheel op de Santa Monica Pier in California. Het werd in 1996 gebouwd en in 1998 omgebouwd tot het eerste reuzenrad op zonne-energie. In de 20 gondels hebben miljoenen mensen van het uitzicht op de Stille Oceaan kunnen genieten – tot het in 2008 door een nieuw reuzenrad werd vervangen. Het oude, maar goed bewaard gebleven reuzenrad werd op eBay verkocht voor een prikje: $ 130.000.

your name on mount mckinley

January 2006, eBay online

© Fotolia, Galyna Andrushko

$ 51

Who wouldn't like to have his or her name on one of the best-known mountains in the world? Well, one young man offered just that on eBay: He intended to climb Mount McKinley and was looking for sponsors to finance his costly mountain expedition. In return, he offered to urinate the sponsors' names into a snow-drift on the mountain! Apparently few sponsors were attracted to this kind of honor, because the highest bid amounted to a meager $ 51. Whether that was enough for the young man to even start out on his tour is anybody's guess...

Qui n'aimerait pas voir son nom inscrit sur l'un des sommets les plus connus du monde ? Un jeune homme proposa cette prestation sur eBay : il souhaitait escalader le mont McKinley et recherchait encore des sponsors pour ce projet à gros budget – en échange, il proposait d'écrire le nom du sponsor en faisant pipi sur une congère de cette montagne ! Cet honneur n'attira pas les foules de sponsors, car la plus haute enchère n'atteignit guère que 51 dollars. On ignore si le jeune homme put réaliser son expédition avec cette somme…

Wie wil er zijn of haar naam niet op een van de bekendste bergen te wereld zien staan? Een jongeman stelde precies dat voor op eBay: hij zou de Mount Mc-Kinley beklimmen en was op zoek naar sponsors om zijn dure bergexpeditie te financieren. In ruil daarvoor zou hij de naam van zijn sponsors in de bergsneeuw plassen! Blijkbaar waren er maar weinig sponsors voor te vinden; het hoogste bod bedroeg amper $ 51. Maar of dat genoeg was om zelfs maar aan zijn expeditie te beginnen...

© Fotolia, rcaucino

the sexiest millenium party ever

December 1999, Playboy, online

$1,800

What man has never dreamed of being there with Hugh Hefner and his Bunnies whenever they party down at the famous-notorious Playboy Mansion? In December 1999, that dream became reality for one lucky guy: 1,800 bucks made him the highest bidder for a ticket to what was likely the hottest Millennium party of all time—a hang out with the legendary Hugh Hefner, lots of gorgeous playmates and upcoming stars, who are always partial to having a good time at the Playboy Mansion.

Quel homme n'a pas rêvé d'être parmi les hôtes des soirées débridées organisées par Hugh Hefner avec ses Bunnies dans la mythique Playboy Mansion ? Pour un chanceux, ce rêve est devenu réalité en décembre 1999 : pour 1 800 dollars, le meilleur enchérisseur obtint son ticket d'entrée à la soirée de la Saint Sylvestre du millénaire probablement la plus torride de tous les temps – aux côtés du légendaire Hugh Hefner, de nombreuses ravissantes playmates et de célébrités en vue qui aiment toujours faire la fête dans la villa Playboy.

Welke man heeft er nog nooit van gedroomd om samen met Hugh Hefner en zijn Bunnies een feestje te bouwen in de beroemde en beruchte Playboy Mansion? In december van 1999 werd die droom alvast voor één gelukzak werkelijkheid: met 1.800 dollar bracht hij het hoogste bod uit op een ticket voor wat waarschijnlijk het meest zinderende millenniumfeestje aller tijden was – een onderonsje met de legendarische Hugh Hefner, tal van bloedmooie playmates en rijzende sterren, die altijd wel te vinden zijn voor een feestje in de Playboy Mansion.

© Getty Images